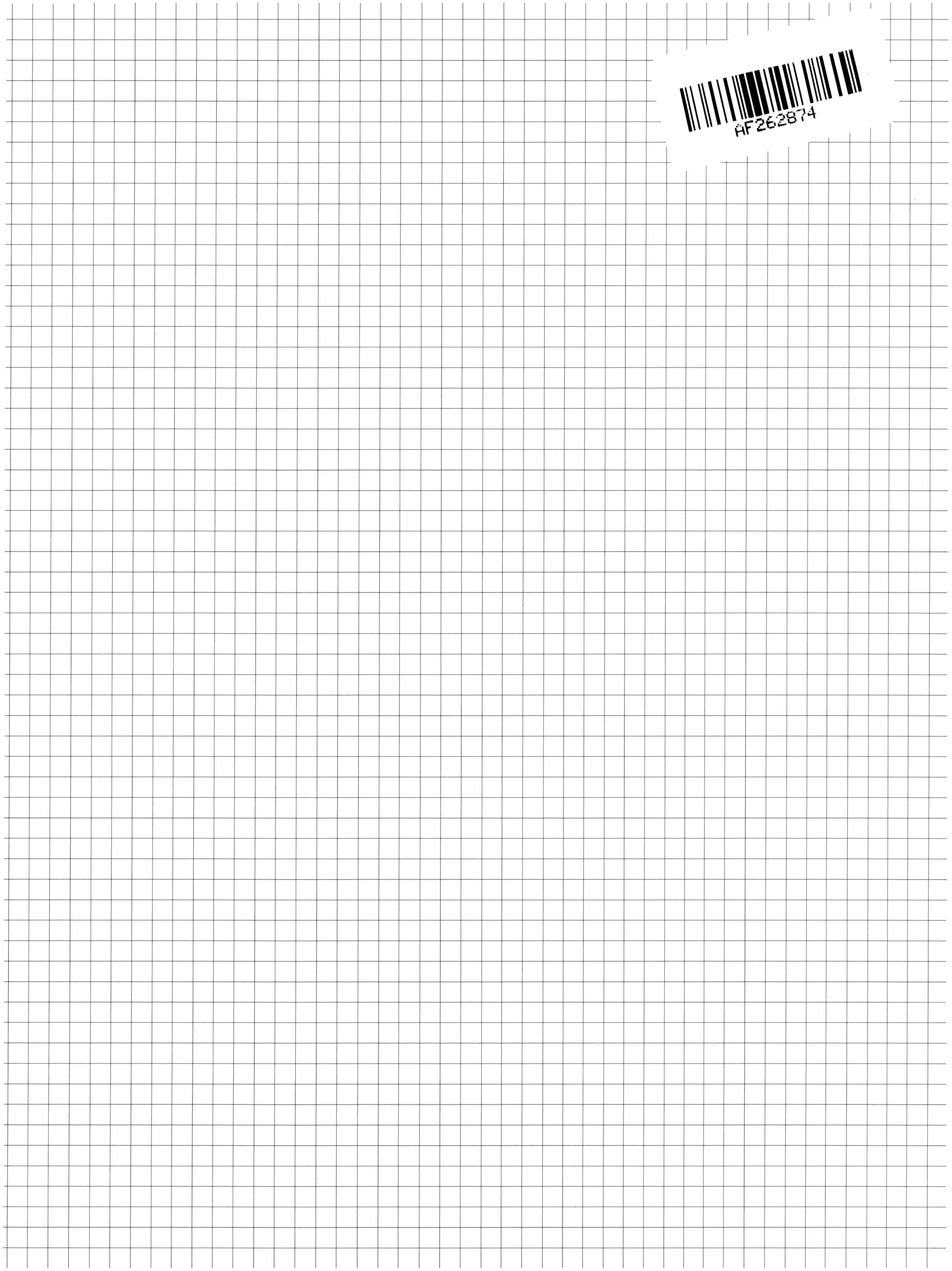
AF262874

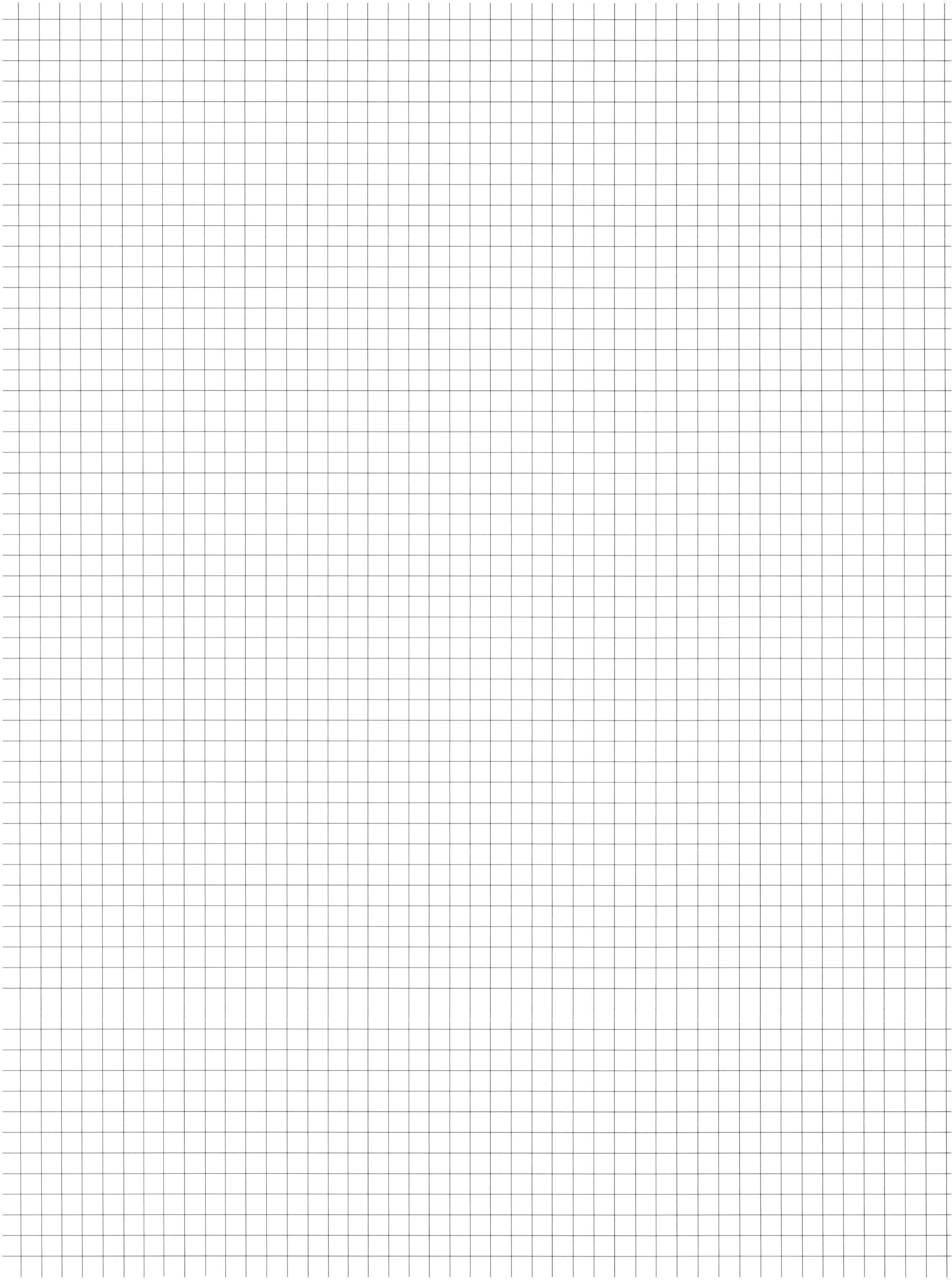

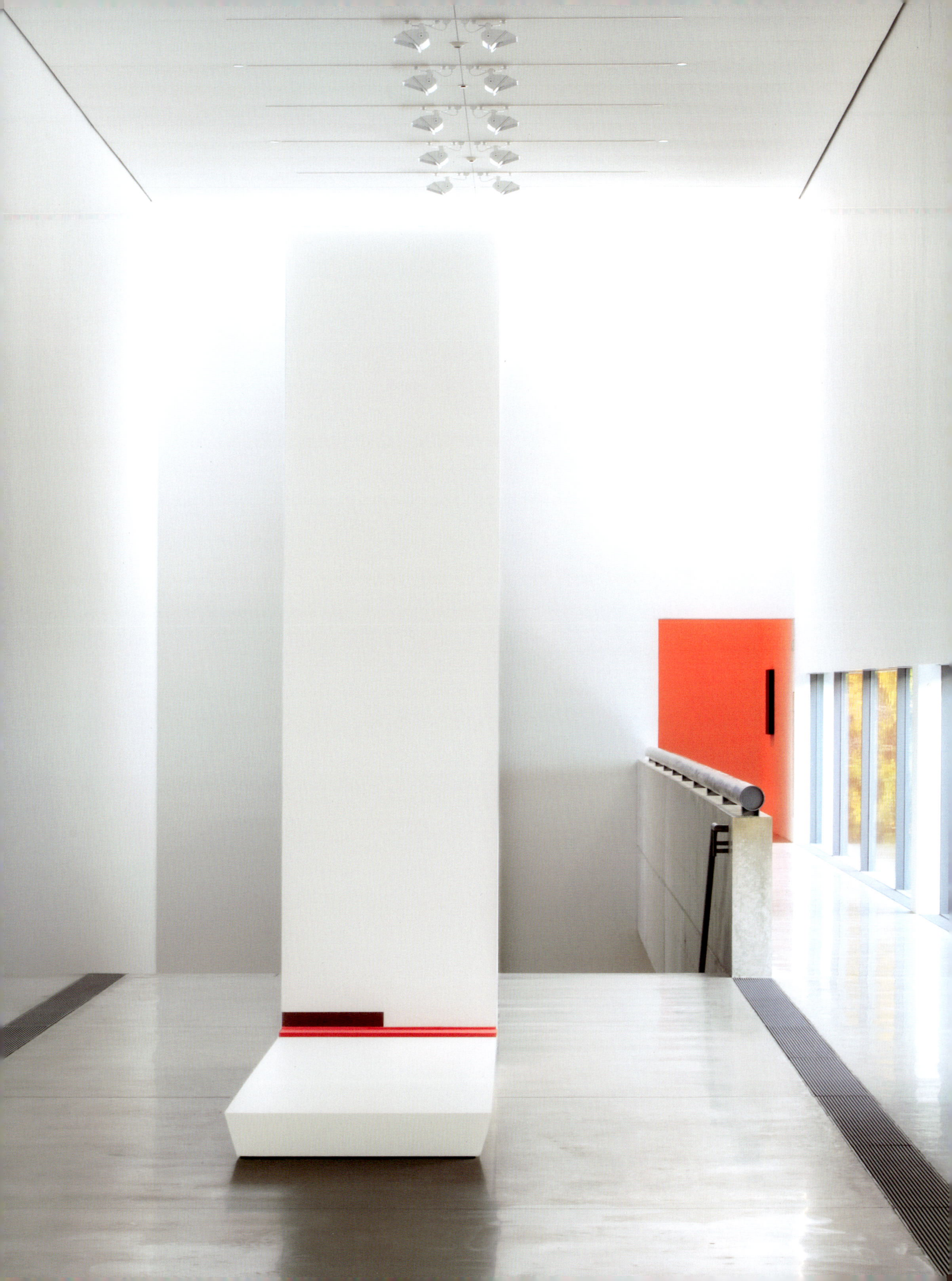

Stephanie Weissberg with Heather Alexis Smith

Pulitzer Arts Foundation

JENNIE   C.

                         JONES

                    A

                                        LINE

WHEN

                          BROKEN

          BEGINS

                          AGAIN

Select writings on artists by Jennie C. Jones

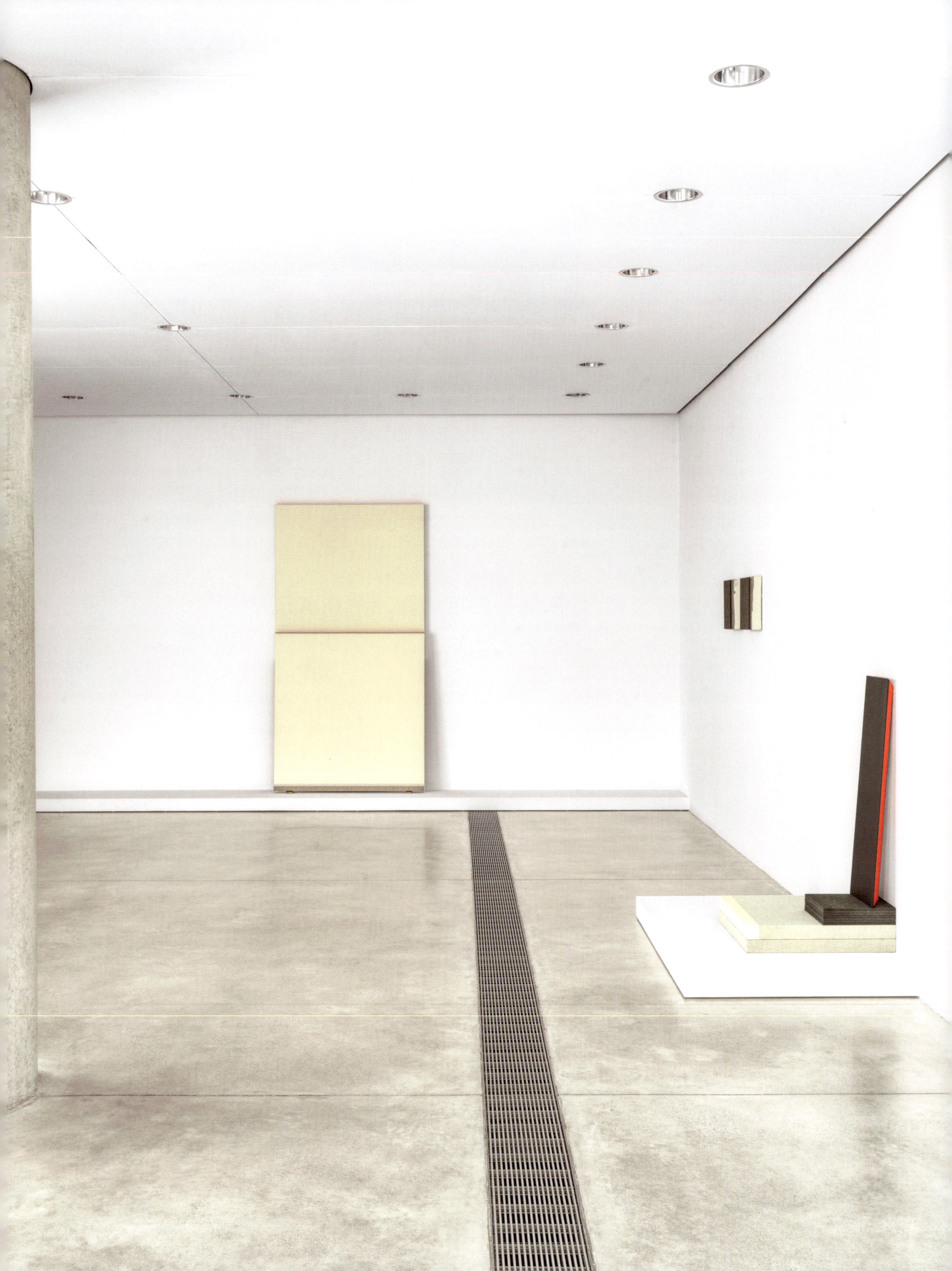

Director's Foreword

Jennie C. Jones calls our attention to the spaces that surround us. Assembling nontraditional materials like felt, acoustic paneling, and instrument strings into refined, abstract works, Jones heightens our senses of sight and sound while deepening our engagement with architecture and environment. The austere geometry and refined hues of her paintings and sculptures are grounded in Conceptualism, Minimalism, and Black experimental sonic traditions. These qualities coalesce in *A Line When Broken Begins Again*, which features new and existing paintings, sculptures, and works on paper by Jones. True to form, the works situate themselves in a sensitive dialogue with the Pulitzer's Tadao Ando–designed building, asking us to see and feel each space in a new light. Jones's site-specific sculpture *Point of Perspective* animates the museum's main gallery, engaging Ellsworth Kelly's monumental wall sculpture *Blue Black* in a conversation that holds personal and art historical resonances.

This occasion also marks a milestone for Jones: her debut as a curator. With *Other Octaves*, she has assembled twenty artists, most of whom worked in the United States during the 1960s and 1970s. These artists are of personal importance, shedding unprecedented light on the "many gifts, insights, and inspiration[s]" they have provided to Jones. They also left foundational marks on the history of twentieth-century art, because, in the words of Jones, they "followed their paths; added a disruption or a counterpoint to the main dialogues of their era." *Other Octaves* reveals surprising connections between these figures, many of whom explored the expressive potential of systems, materiality, fragility, color, and geometry. My warmest congratulations to Jones on the achievement of these two exhibitions.

Stephanie Weissberg, senior curator, worked tirelessly to bring these exhibitions to life, and she is a passionate champion of the artist's vision as well as a sensitive and thoughtful collaborator. Also invaluable were Heather Alexis Smith, assistant curator, who contributed to all aspects of this project and catalogue, along with Katie DiDomenico, Christopher Hunt, and Adrianne Koteen for their research support. Finally, I want to acknowledge Jones's representatives at Alexander Gray Associates, and especially Page Benkowski and John Kunemund, for their outstanding advocacy and assistance.

For generously lending works to *A Line When Broken Begins Again* and *Other Octaves*, I am grateful to Alexander Gray, owner and principal, and David Cabrera, owner and principal, Alexander Gray Associates; Mr. and Mrs. Lee Broughton; Jacqueline Terrassa, Carolyn Muzzy Director, Colby Museum of Art; Jessica Morgan, director, Dia Art Foundation; Steve Elmendorf; Mary Miller, former director, Getty Research Institute; The JLS Collection; Jennie C. Jones; Lizbeth and George Krupp; Alex Logsdail, chief executive officer, Lisson Gallery; Glenn D. Lowry, former David Rockefeller Director, and Christophe Cherix, current David Rockefeller Director, The Museum of Modern Art, New York; Kaywin Feldman, director, National Gallery of Art; Susan M. Taylor, The Montine McDaniel Freeman Director, New Orleans Museum of Art; Claudia Volpe, director and curator, Petrucci Family Foundation Collection of African American Art; Jack Shear; Bill Goldston and Larissa Goldston, owners/directors, Universal Limited Art Editions; Alex Nyerges, director and chief executive officer, Virginia Museum of Fine Arts; Scott Rothkopf, Alice Pratt Brown Director, Whitney Museum of American Art; and those lenders who wish to remain anonymous.

No project is possible without the efforts of the Pulitzer's incredible staff. In addition to our devoted colleagues on the Pulitzer's curatorial, public engagement, and marketing and communications teams, I recognize Laura Blumenberg, assistant registrar; Natalie M. Foster, director of registration and exhibition management; Steve Gibbs, lead preparator; and Shane Simmons, director of exhibition design and installation, for their dedication to these exhibitions.

Many others brought this catalogue to life. I extend my appreciation to Katy Nelson, for her thoughtful and sensitive design; Donna Wingate and Susan Larsen, for their expert editorial insight; and the team at Marquand Books who ushered the catalogue into being: Gina Broze, Leah Finger, Ryan Polich, and Kestrel Rundle.

Finally, my thanks goes to the Board of Directors of the Pulitzer Arts Foundation, and especially to Emily Rauh Pulitzer, founder and chair of the board. Your support is a constant inspiration that makes our work possible. Thank you.

Cara Starke
Executive Director
Pulitzer Arts Foundation

POINT OF PERSPECTIVE

STEPHANIE WEISSBERG

Jennie C. Jones makes paintings, sculpture, works on paper, and sound installations that engage the histories of the avant-garde in visual art and music, with a particular focus on Minimalism and Black experimental sonic traditions. She has developed a highly distilled visual vocabulary, primarily working with abstract geometric forms and a focused range of colors. Using nontraditional materials, such as architectural felt, acoustic panels, and instrument strings, Jones produces works that modify the acoustics of their environments, thereby amplifying our attention to the spaces that surround us.

Jones gives us subtle cues through her work. Some are physical, beckoning us to lean closer as we perceive a slight dulling of ambient noise while the paintings work to absorb the sound around them. Others are intellectual, prompting us to consider the histories of abstraction and improvisation as they intersect across art and music. These two registers do not function independently in Jones's work but build on each other to create an overall experience that is uniquely rich and nuanced. For her exhibition at the Pulitzer, *A Line When Broken Begins Again*, Jones presents new and existing works that deepen this interplay between the perceptual and conceptual. When considered alongside *Other Octaves*, the concurrent exhibition she has curated for the museum, we are afforded a fuller and more complex understanding of Jones's engagement with material, sound, history, and legacy.

After studying painting at the School of the Art Institute of Chicago and Rutgers University, Jones spent her early career producing sound works, drawings, and sculptures from found materials that consider the history of listening and music culture. In the early 2000s she returned to painting with an interest in "thread[ing] painting, architecture, and acoustics together, to bring my poetic and heartachy love of music history together with the narrative of how American modernism was constructed, which left out American music."[1] For Jones, this new direction was predicated on an understanding of painting not as pictorial representation but as an object within an architectural and acoustical environment. This realization led the artist to develop works that have as much to do with the history of painting as they do sculpture.

Jones's use of sound-absorbing materials to create subtle variations in the sonic environment link her work to Minimalist sculptors such as Robert Morris, who also concerned himself with the perceptual experience of the viewer. Morris's 1965 sculpture *Untitled (Three Ls)* issued a provocation to the notion that sculpture existed as a self-contained object independent from its environment (fig. 1). By placing three identical forms at divergent angles throughout a gallery, Morris created the illusion of differences in scale and shape that were produced by the viewer's perspective as they moved throughout the room. As Morris outlined in his landmark essay *Notes*

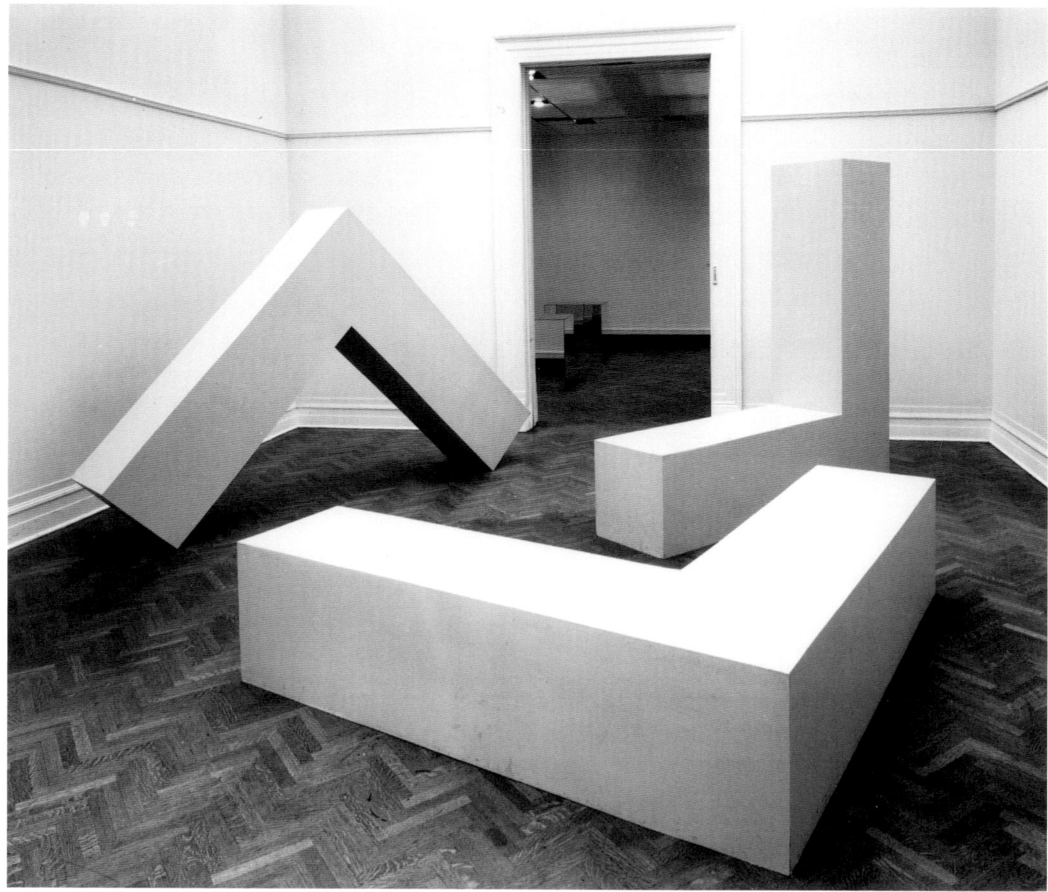

Fig. 1. Robert Morris, *Untitled (Three Ls)*, 1965. Plywood, 8 × 8 × 2 feet.

on Sculpture, "it is the viewer who changes the shape constantly by his change in position relative to the work."[2] Morris's argument for the importance of physicality to the act of meaning making was in part informed by his history as a dancer and choreographer. His earliest Minimal constructions were made as props for performances at Judson Dance Theater. Similarly, the phenomenological aspects of Jones's paintings link the works to the experience of listening to music, which is inherently embodied, perceptual, and temporal.

Jones heightens the perceptual effects of her paintings through subtle and sometimes barely visible shifts in color and surface. After years of exerting exacting control over the surface of her canvases to void them of traces of their making, her more recent experiments with printmaking and the decisive movement of pulling ink across a substrate inspired Jones to embrace gesture in many of her works. She

Fig. 2. Jennie C. Jones, *Pentimenti, Subtone with Soft Sharps* (detail), 2024. Acrylic, acoustic panel, and architectural felt on canvas, 48 × 48 × 2½ inches (121.9 × 121.9 × 6.3 cm). Courtesy Alexander Gray Associates, New York

refers to the marks from her underpaintings that she allows to remain visible as pentimenti, an art historical term that describes the emergence of brushstrokes that have been painted over. The expression points to the close examination required to perceive these shifts, often requiring the viewer to draw near and linger for an extended period. Because her paintings maintain a similar color scheme, format, and scale (they do not exceed four feet in width or height unless they are double-stacked vertically), the slight fluctuations that whisper across the canvases take on an elevated significance. These faint traces are visible in works like *Pentimenti, Subtone with Soft Sharps* (fig. 2), in which wisps of light-cream gray emerge from beneath an overlayer of thicker, cement-colored pigment.

In keeping with what the artist refers to as "a type of deeply personal synesthesia" that is rooted in "seeing sound," Jones likens these pentimenti to the musical

Fig. 3. Jennie C. Jones, *Deep Glissando*, 2021. Acrylic, acoustic panel, and architectural felt on canvas, 48 × 48 × 5 inches (121.9 × 121.9 × 12.7 cm). Courtesy Alexander Gray Associates, New York

technique of the *subtone*, a sound at the lower register of a wind instrument's range, produced by breathing with less pressure than is required to create a full note. The technique is most closely associated with jazz ballads performed by saxophone and clarinet players beginning in the swing era, around 1935. In evoking subtone, Jones makes indirect reference to musicians known for producing its distinctive sound, like saxophonists Harry Carney, who played with the Duke Ellington Orchestra from 1928 to 1974, and Lester Young, whose relaxed, lyrical style influenced a generation of jazz musicians, including Charlie Parker.

Jones continues to layer conceptual references into her work through the language of musical notation. In works like *Pentimenti, Subtone with Soft Sharps*, *Soft End Measure*, and *Deep Glissando* (fig. 3), Jones uses form, composition, and color to reference musical principles and their visual representations in scores. *Deep Glissando*, for instance, is a square canvas split into four vertical bands of irregular widths, each with varying shades of black and gray. Jones achieved the differences of color and texture across the segments by employing a range of materials, including, from left to right, acoustic paneling, architectural felt, and painted canvas. The result is a rhythmic painting that loosely resembles bars on sheet music, a device she has incorporated into a number of her works, most explicitly in collages like *Standing and Moving #1–2* and *#6* (pages 74, 75, and 73). In its central panel, *Deep Glissando* features a downward-sloping line constructed from architectural felt. The form acts as a visual approximation of a *glissando*, a slide from a high to low pitch, and resembles the musical notation used to indicate the technique. The left half of the composition is dominated by a wedge of acoustical paneling that creates a second downward-sloping line when viewed from the side. The dark-toned painting absorbs light, raising associations with low, muffled tones that contrast with the bright reverberating "hum" of red that emanates from the edges of many of her works (page 6).

Likening her process to a walkabout through history, Jones often puts the figures and movements she references in her work into dialogue with the surrounding architectural and art historical context. At the Clark Art Institute, she produced a sculptural intervention that extended from the concrete arm of the museum's outdoor pavilion, designed by Tadao Ando (also the architect of the Pulitzer). Jones's work acted as a functioning Aeolian harp that produced sound when activated by the wind, referencing Alice Coltrane's signature instrument. At the Hirshhorn Museum, she installed a sound work sampling music by experimental jazz luminaries, including Wendell Logan and the Association for the Advancement of Creative Musicians, with the intention of allowing the sounds to drift into adjacent galleries featuring work by Ellsworth Kelly and Clyfford Still.

At the Pulitzer, Jones's paintings are on view alongside her first freestanding sculpture for an interior space. The work acts as an homage and a provocation, combining the phenomenological and conceptual to prompt us to reconsider our perceptions of space and history. Titled *Point of Perspective* (frontispiece and page 119), the sculpture occupies the center of the museum's main gallery, where it engages Kelly's monumental wall sculpture *Blue Black*, on permanent view at one end of the room. The two works have several formal similarities. They share the same vertical to horizontal ratio and flat application of color, and both apply the language of abstract painting to sculpture. *Point of Perspective* comprises two flat planes that meet at a right angle. One projects straight upward while the other stretches horizontally across the floor. This form relates to an earlier work by Kelly, *Blue White Angle* (1966), which he cited as a point of inspiration for *Blue Black*. Jones's new work hews closely to the visual vernacular the artist has developed through her paintings with restrained color and geometry and the application of sound-absorbing bass traps. This material choice links the sculpture to the artist's paintings, where her use of industrially produced, sound-absorbing media challenges the idea of pictorial representation and instead emphasizes the works' materiality.

As Jones notes, her work is rooted in "thinking about painting as an object rather than painting as a window. Paintings are indeed objects in rooms, and those rooms have acoustic properties."[3] Though Kelly did not actively concern himself with acoustics in producing his work, he did place great importance on the relationship between his paintings and the surrounding architecture. In a 1950 letter to composer John Cage, he explained, "My collages are only ideas for things much larger—things to cover walls.…I am not interested in painting as it has been accepted for so long—to hang on the walls of houses as pictures. To hell with pictures—they should *be* the wall."[4] Beginning in the 1950s, he produced increasingly ambitious relief paintings as well as wall and freestanding sculptures. By 1990 he produced his first floor sculpture, *Yellow Curve*, which occupied nearly the entire footprint at Portikus Frankfurt, forcing viewers to contend with its obstructing presence (fig. 4).[5]

Of the many figures who brought painting into the realm of the spatial and perceptual, two stand out for their importance to Jones. By 1959, Carmen Herrera, who was trained in architecture, began applying paint to the edges of the painting, initializing a break between it and the wall (page 68). A decade later, she began realizing work that complicated the relationship between painting, sculpture, and architecture. Originally conceived as three-dimensional extensions of her hard-edge abstract paintings, Herrera's monochromatic *Estructuras* (Structures) use negative space to implicate the surrounding environment. The white walls

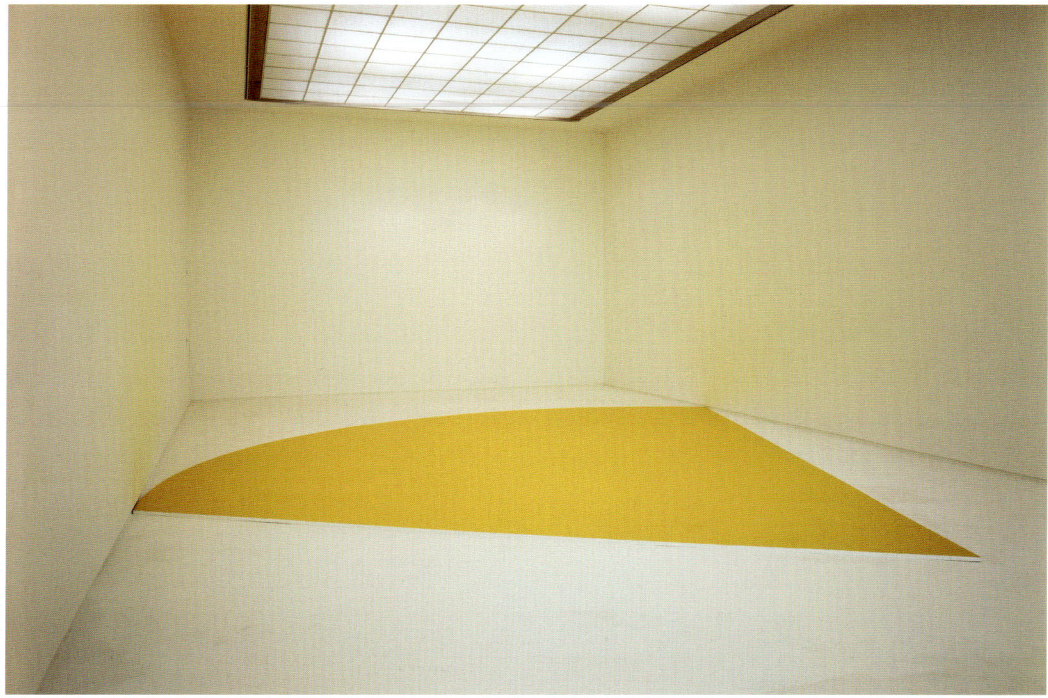

Fig. 4. Ellsworth Kelly, *Yellow Curve*, 1990. Acrylic on canvas on wood, 1 × 283 × 312 inches.

exposed through irregular gaps in the work become a secondary color in her sculptural compositions. Beginning in the early 1960s, Anne Truitt was making upright, nonrepresentational painted wood sculptures in which she used color as an index for memories and emotional states. She later wrote of her freestanding sculptures, "I slowly came to realize, that what I was actually trying to do was to take paintings off the wall, to set color free in three-dimensions for its own sake."[6] Truitt painstakingly applied layers of paint to produce slight shifts in hue across her sculptures, thereby producing complex optical and perceptual effects as the viewer moves around the work.

With *Point of Perspective*, Jones brings her work off the wall into the center of the gallery, as Morris, Kelly, Truitt, and Herrera did before her. By presenting an object that the viewer must contend with in physical space rather than solely as a frontal plane, Jones heightens the sensory and experiential dimensions of her work. As a viewer walks into the long, narrow gallery, she sees *Point of Perspective* in the foreground and, alongside it, *Blue Black* in the background. As she moves toward the center of the space, Kelly's sculpture becomes eclipsed, disappearing behind Jones's. This vanishing effect only lasts for a brief moment while the viewer occupies a specific location, dependent on their own eye level. Once she continues on her path to the left or right, *Blue Black* appears again. As one traverses the gallery, the two works seem to be linked in a synchronized dance in which one steps in front while the other dips behind, then back around on the other side, always in motion.

For Jones, this dance extends back to her early development as an artist at the School of the Art Institute of Chicago, where she earned a BFA in 1991. In the years she attended school there, the Art Institute of Chicago commissioned and installed six aluminum wall sculptures by Kelly for a prominent rotunda adjacent to their American art galleries. For the young artist, the celebration of Kelly and the resulting displacement of other artists whose work had been on view elicited complex emotions. While she was moved by the crisp elegance of Kelly's forms, the installation also raised questions for her about whose voices were brought to the fore and who was afforded the privilege of concerning oneself with pure form and color. These questions were especially salient for Jones at a moment when heightened pressure for Black artists to make representational work that engaged with the identity politics of the moment felt constraining to her and many of her peers.

Charles Gaines addresses this pressure in the catalogue accompanying his landmark 1993 exhibition *The Theater of Refusal: Black Art and Mainstream Criticism*. He argues that postmodern theory failed Black artists by championing "difference," only to collapse work made by Black artists into a monolithic group defined by its relationship to the White mainstream.[7] While Gaines's text addresses this condition in relation to visual art, it was true across creative disciplines, including music. The text was published the year Jones began her graduate work at Rutgers and significantly influenced the discourse around marginality during her studies. Gaines outlines the trap of many postmodern theories that position the marginal and mainstream as a dialectical pair, such as "self/other," thereby relegating the marginal to the role of defining the boundaries of the mainstream. He argues instead for the concept of "becoming" theorized by Gilles Deleuze and Félix Guattari. Their theory describes a means of negotiating marginality through the process of actively differentiating from the mainstream, called deterritorialization. This undertaking transforms both the minority and majority and involves a process of ongoing negotiation and self-definition called becoming that is imbued with the "conflict and contradiction" inherent in real lived experiences.

Point of Perspective might be interpreted as a form of becoming that allows Jones to carve out space for a more complex way of being in relation to the history of painting and abstraction. This negotiation is nuanced and sometimes contradictory in the way deeply personal experiences often are. On one level, the gesture

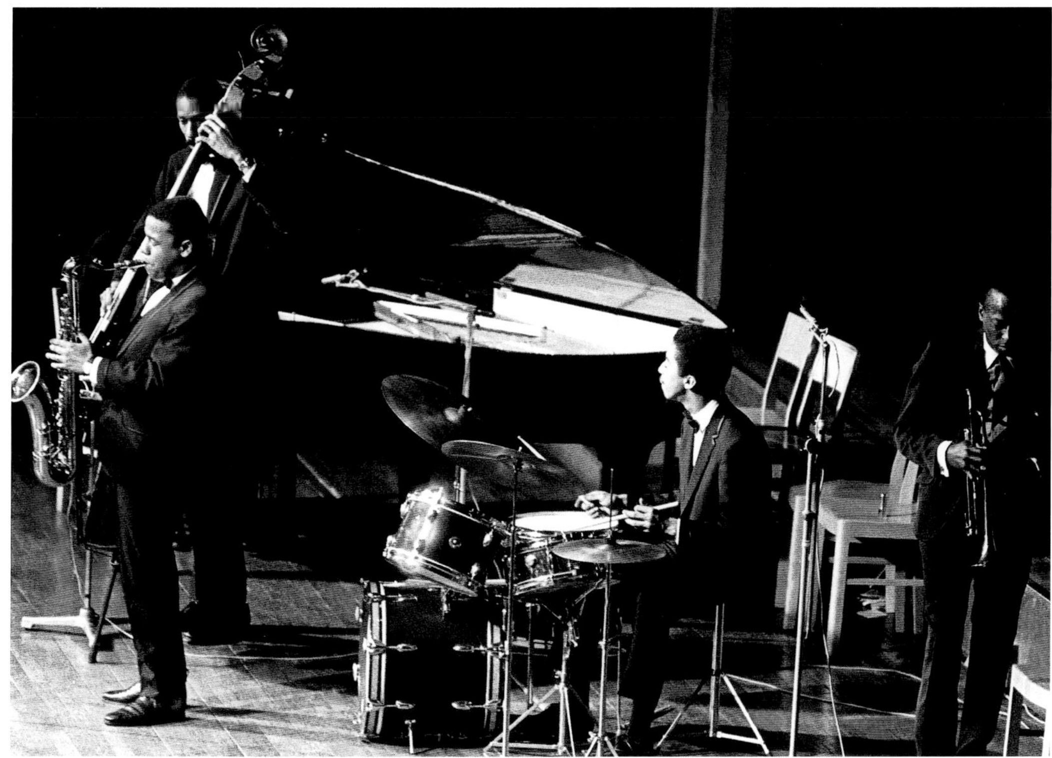

Fig. 5. Miles Davis Quartet, Wayne Shorter (sax), Ron Carter (bass), Tony Williams (drums), Miles Davis (trumpet), Copenhagen Jazz Festival, 1964.

pays homage to Kelly, acknowledging his significance to the room and to art history at large. Simultaneously, by orienting the face of *Point of Perspective* toward the entrance of the gallery rather than to *Blue Black* at its rear, Jones avoids direct engagement with Kelly.

This staging brings to mind the story of an iconic gesture from music history. By at least the late 1950s, Miles Davis was known to turn his back on the audience during performances. This posture has often been interpreted as an attitude of aloof disinterest or an outright refusal to cater to expectations that a musician's primary concern should be the experience of the audience. In a 1984 interview, Davis couched his movement as a pursuit of musical excellence, explaining that he repositioned his body throughout his performances in order to find the optimum angle to produce the most ideal sonic qualities for each instrument and note. He went on to add, "I always try to pick the best spot…where I can hear myself, that's really what's happening" (fig. 5).[8] While Davis was addressing his ability to hear himself, and his bandmates, in literal terms, his comment also functions on a metaphorical level. In order to fully realize his authentic sound, he needed to cleave his attention from the conventions of musical performance and the expectations of the audience. Like Davis, Jones's act of turning away from and eclipsing Kelly is not an outright denial or repudiation but rather a means of momentarily turning the volume down on the loudest voices in the canon in order to hear what she refers to as "other octaves"—including her own and those referenced in her work—more clearly.

While Jones negotiates her positioning in relation to Kelly with *Point of Perspective*, she does not share Davis's relationship with her own audience. Although her sculpture steadfastly holds space in the center of the gallery, it is not until the viewer enters the room that the conversation begins. As the title indicates, *Point of Perspective* is dependent on the engagement of the viewer, who becomes both an onlooker in a dialogue between Jones and Kelly and a member of an ensemble who performs alongside them as she moves throughout the space. As with Robert Morris's *Untitled (Three Ls)*, the underpinnings of the work have been predetermined by the artist, but they require embodied experience on the part of the viewer to be fully realized. Jones not only makes the physical movement throughout space critical to the understanding of her work, but she also roots the conceptual conceit of the installation in the perspective of the viewer. While this move represents a new dimension of the perceptual in her work, it is not an end in itself. Rather, the artist focuses our awareness on the details of our surroundings— including the architecture and art and their attendant histories—to pose questions about whose voices are centered and whose are sidelined.

At the Pulitzer, Jones is extending her historical walkabouts beyond the scope of her own work to a curatorial endeavor for the first time. Her exhibition, *Other Octaves*, does not trace a linear timeline but instead identifies moments of harmony across disparate approaches to material, form, and color. Jones identifies resonances in the work of Agnes Martin, Alma Thomas, and Anne Truitt, who each possess the ability to convey complex emotional states with remarkable visual economy and subtle variations in color. She brings our attention to the immediacy of experiments with paper, even among artists who are more well known for their work in painting and sculpture. Drawings, collages, and prints by Zarina Hashmi, Louise Nevelson, Martin Puryear, and Mavis Pusey, among others, share a sense of rhythm and tactility imbued from the rough edges of torn paper or the graphic imprint of black ink. A literal sense of musicality appears in drawings, scores, and performance documentation by Benjamin Patterson, Hanne Darboven, and Julius Eastman. Jones also asks us to indulge in the perceptual prompts issued by artists like Carmen Herrera and Fred Eversley, who invite us to look through and move around their work in order to inform our understanding of the space around us. The result is a poetic and open-ended reshuffling of the art historical deck that extends Jones's career-long project of gently directing our gaze to consider other perspectives.

1   "Jennie C. Jones by Lauren Haynes," *BOMB*, September 16, 2024, https://bombmagazine.org /articles/2024/09/16/jennie-c-jones-lauren-haynes.

2   Robert Morris, "Notes on Sculpture, Part 2," *Artforum* (October 1966): 20–23.

3   "Jennie C. Jones by Lauren Haynes."

4   Tricia Y. Paik, "In France 1948–54," in *Ellsworth Kelly*, ed. Tricia Y. Paik (Phaidon, 2015), 44.

5   The sentiment Kelly expressed in his letter to Cage represents an emerging investment among artists in spatializing painting. In 1964, Donald Judd addressed this growing tendency in his essay "Specific Objects," writing, "Half or more of the best new work in the last few years has been neither painting nor sculpture. Usually it has been related, closely or distantly, to one or the other." Though Judd acknowledged that this new work did not constitute a specific movement or style, the considerations he outlined have become most commonly associated with Minimalism. They were, however, also being forwarded by artists who were sidelined by or themselves rejected the movement due to divergent concerns.

6   Anne Truitt, *Daybook: The Journal of an Artist* (Pantheon Books, 1982), 81.

7   As curator Valerie Cassel Oliver points out, while all artists, regardless of race and gender, who make work that challenges status quo risk obscurity, the few who came to be recognized as the progenitors of contemporary art, beginning in the 1960s, were by and large White and male.

8   "City Line: Miles Davis," December 2, 1984, WJZ-TV, Baltimore. Video posted June 6, 2021, https://archive.org/details/WJZ-CTYLN-003–002.

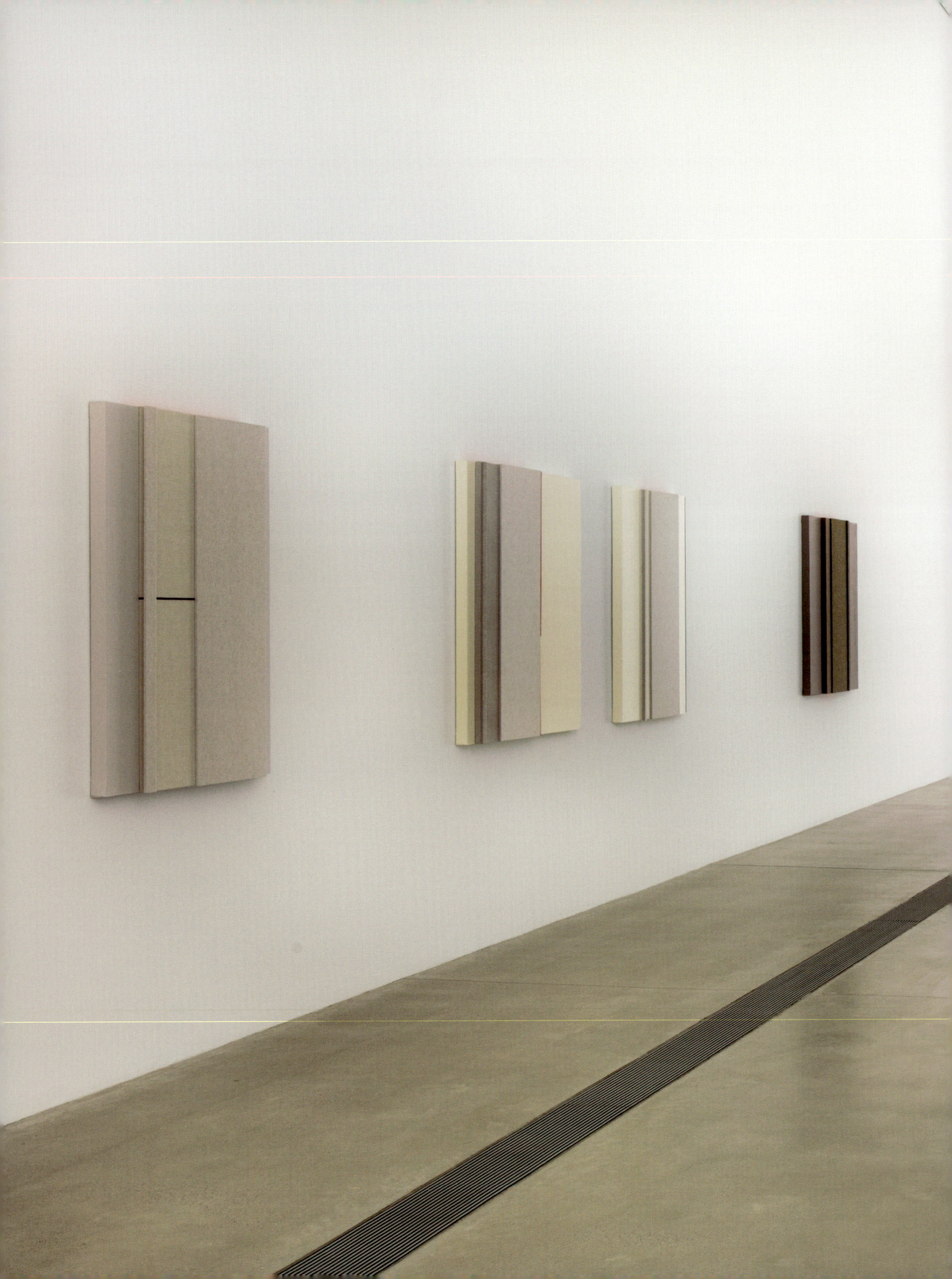

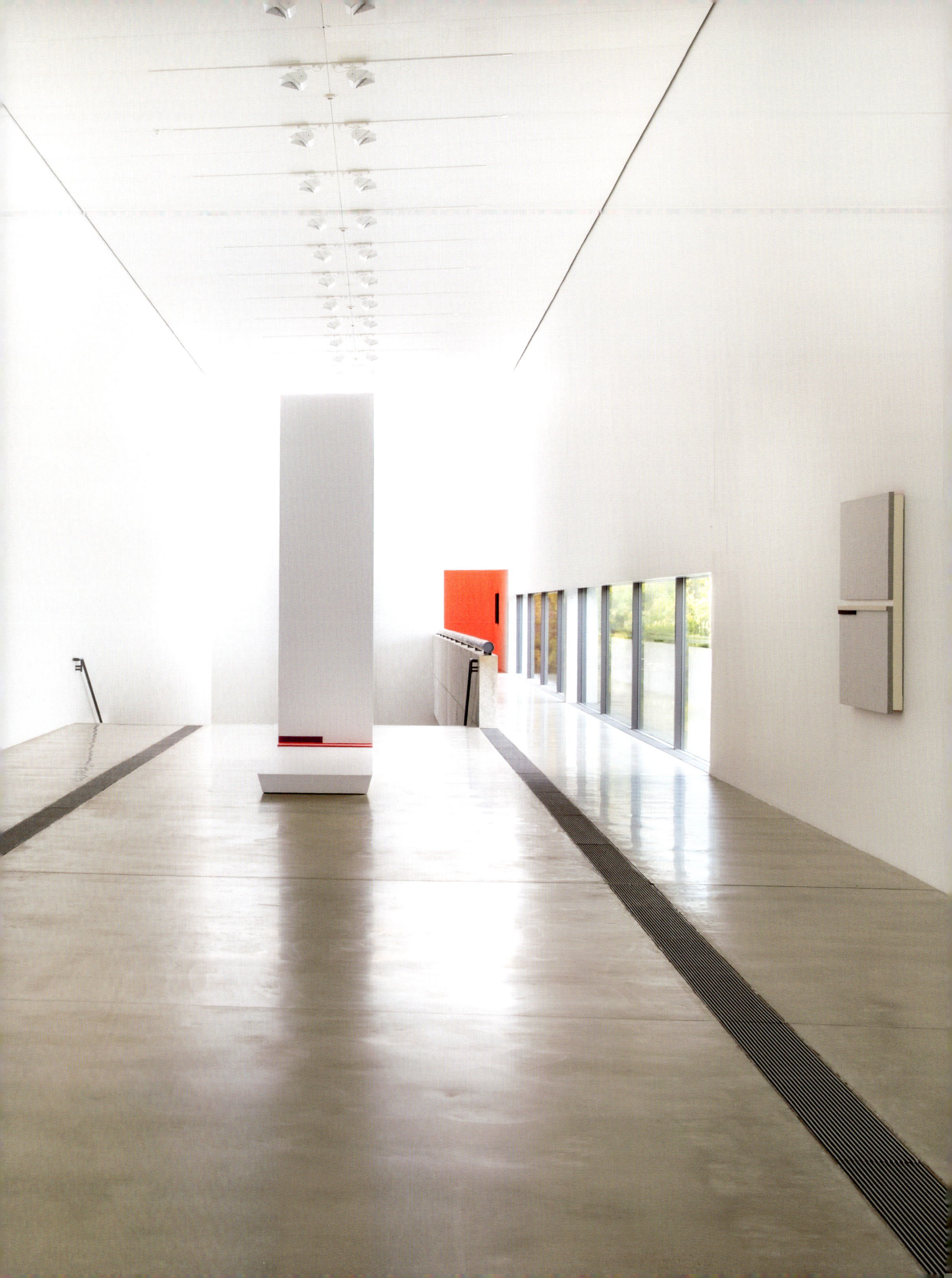

Jennie C. Jones, *Triple Bold Bar, End Measure*, 2022
Acrylic, acoustic panel, and architectural felt on canvas in 2 parts, 48 × 48 × 3½ inches (121.9 × 121.9 × 8.9 cm) each
Courtesy Alexander Gray Associates, New York

Jennie C. Jones, *Soft Sharps, Line Break,* 2023
Acrylic, acoustic panel, and architectural felt on canvas, 48 × 36⅛ × 3⅛ inches (121.9 × 91.8 × 7.9 cm)
The JLS Collection

Jennie C. Jones, *Deep Red, Black*, 2025
Acrylic, acoustic panel, and architectural felt on board,
30 × 30⅜ × 2½ inches (76.2 × 77.2 × 6.4 cm)
Courtesy Alexander Gray Associates, New York

Jennie C. Jones, *Hushed with Black Red Edge*, 2025
Acrylic, acoustic panel, and architectural felt on canvas,
48 × 36⅜ × 2¾ inches (121.9 × 92.4 × 7 cm)
Courtesy Alexander Gray Associates, New York

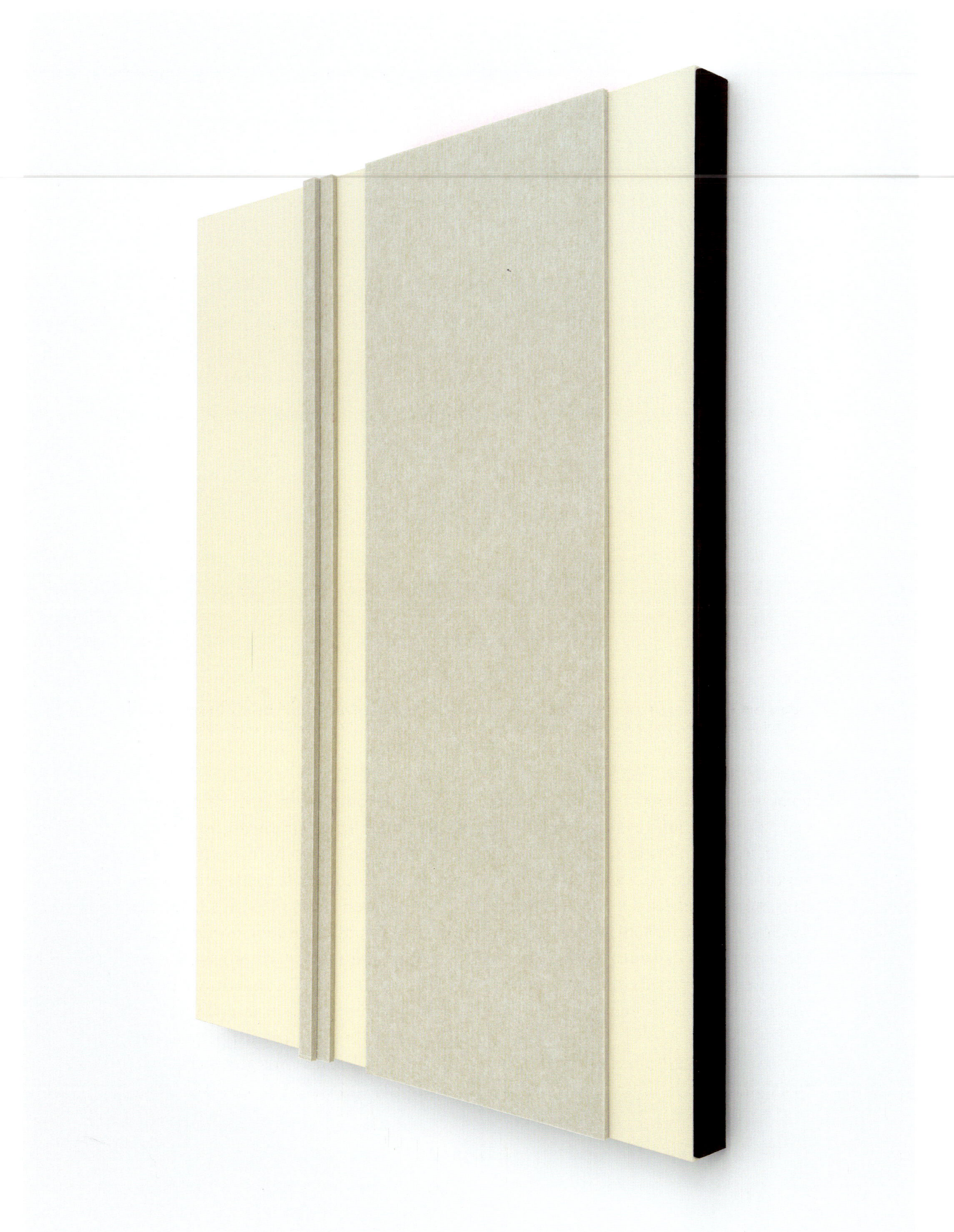

Jennie C. Jones, *Phrasing to the Floor, Softly, as in an Evening Sunset (for Nina)*, **2025**
Acrylic and architectural felt on canvas and brass in 4 parts, part 1: 48½ × 48 × 2½ inches (123.2 × 121.9 × 6.4 cm);
part 2: 48 × 48 × 2 inches (121.9 × 121.9 × 5.1 cm); 2 brass blocks: 2 × 2 inches (5.1 × 5.1 cm) each
Courtesy Alexander Gray Associates, New York

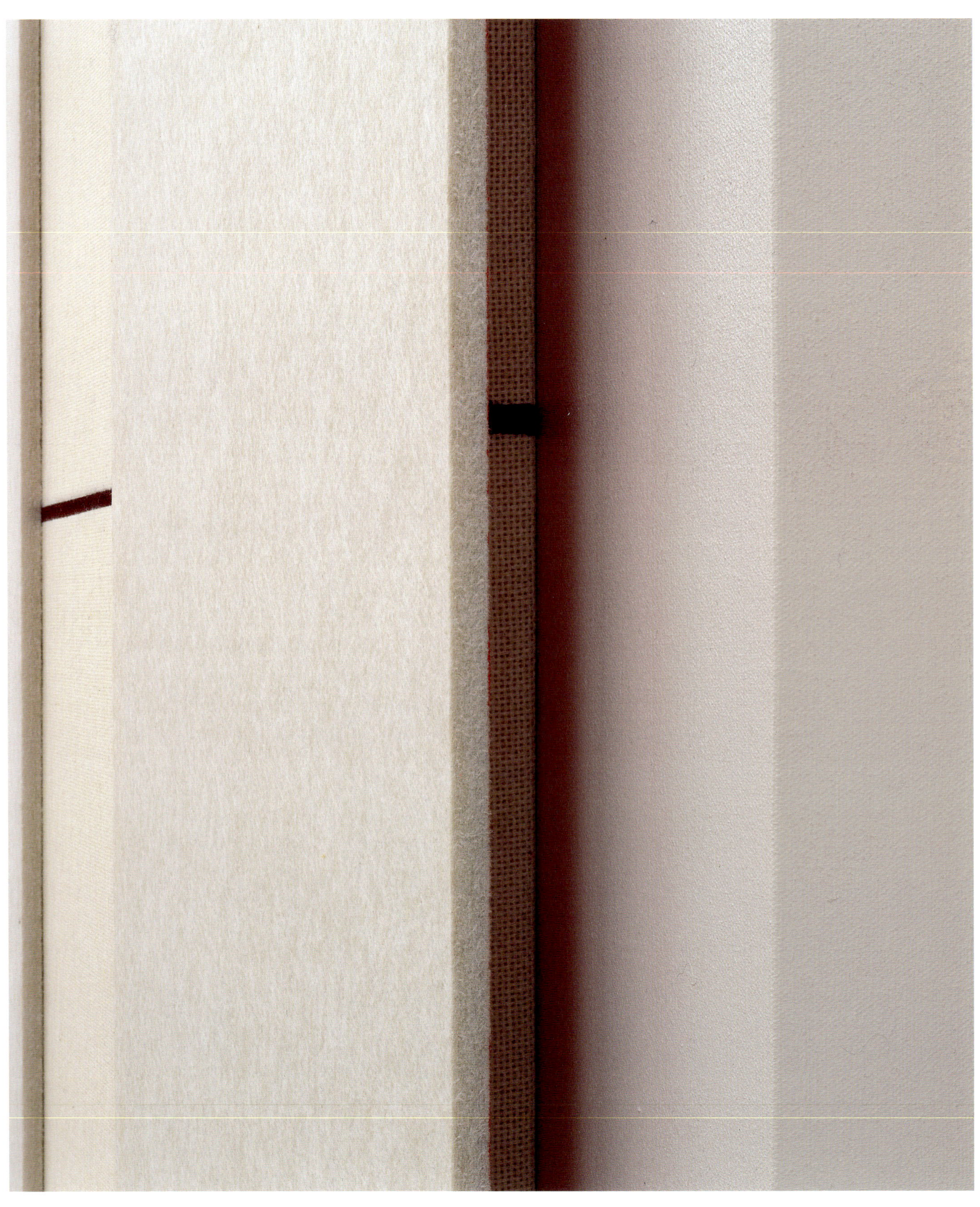

Jennie C. Jones, *A Line When Broken***, 2025**
Acrylic, acoustic panel, and architectural felt on canvas, 48 × 36¼ × 3⅝ inches (121.9 × 92.1 × 9.2 cm)
Courtesy Alexander Gray Associates, New York

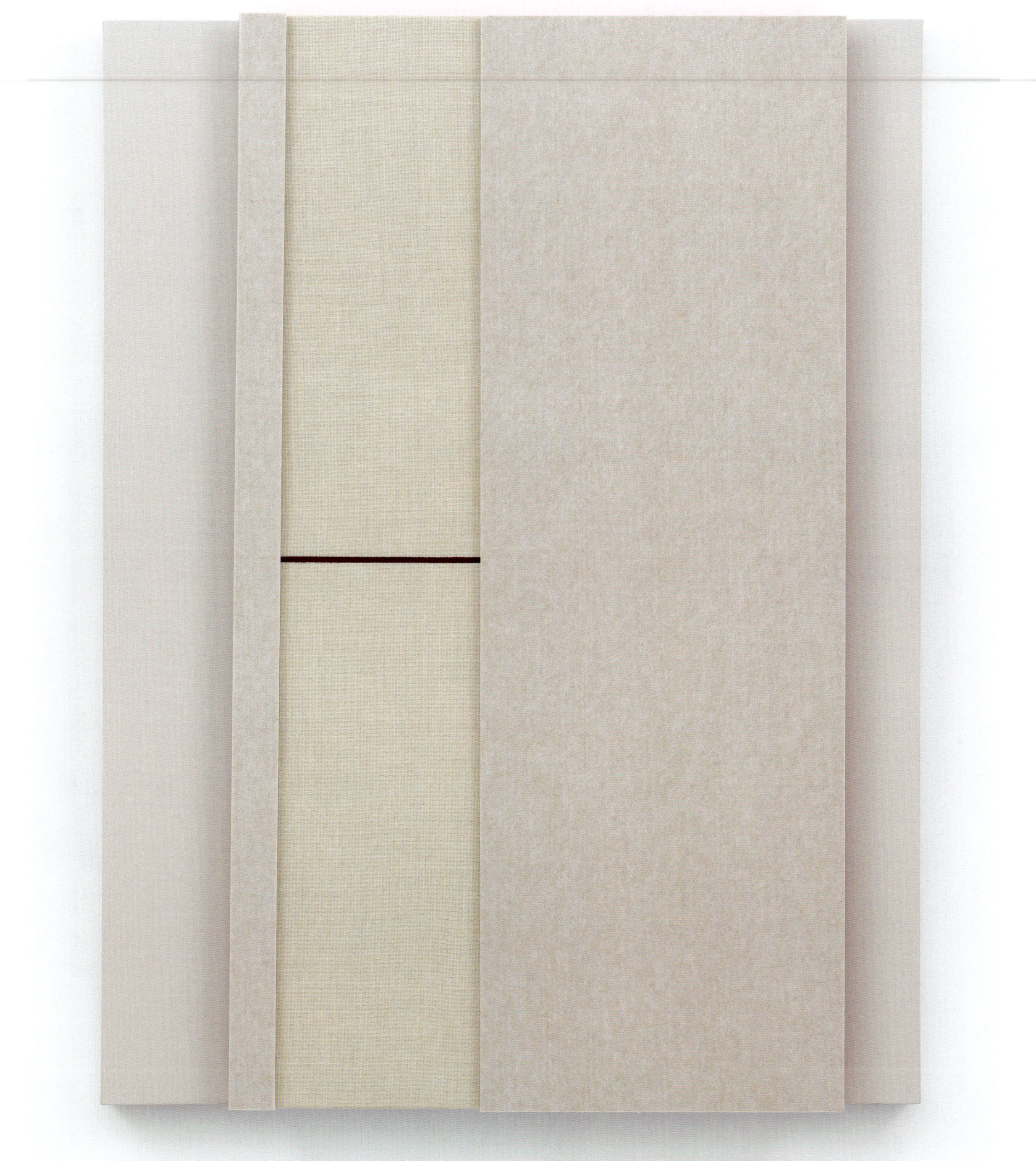

Jennie C. Jones, *Measured Earth Tone*, **2025**
Acrylic, acoustic panel, and architectural felt on canvas, 48 × 48⅛ × 3¾ inches (121.9 × 122.2 × 9.5 cm)
Courtesy Alexander Gray Associates, New York

Jennie C. Jones, *Two Hushed Movements (Diptych)*, **2025**

Acrylic, acoustic panel, and architectural felt on canvas, 12 × 12½ × 2½ inches (30.5 × 31.8 × 6.4 cm) each

Courtesy Alexander Gray Associates, New York

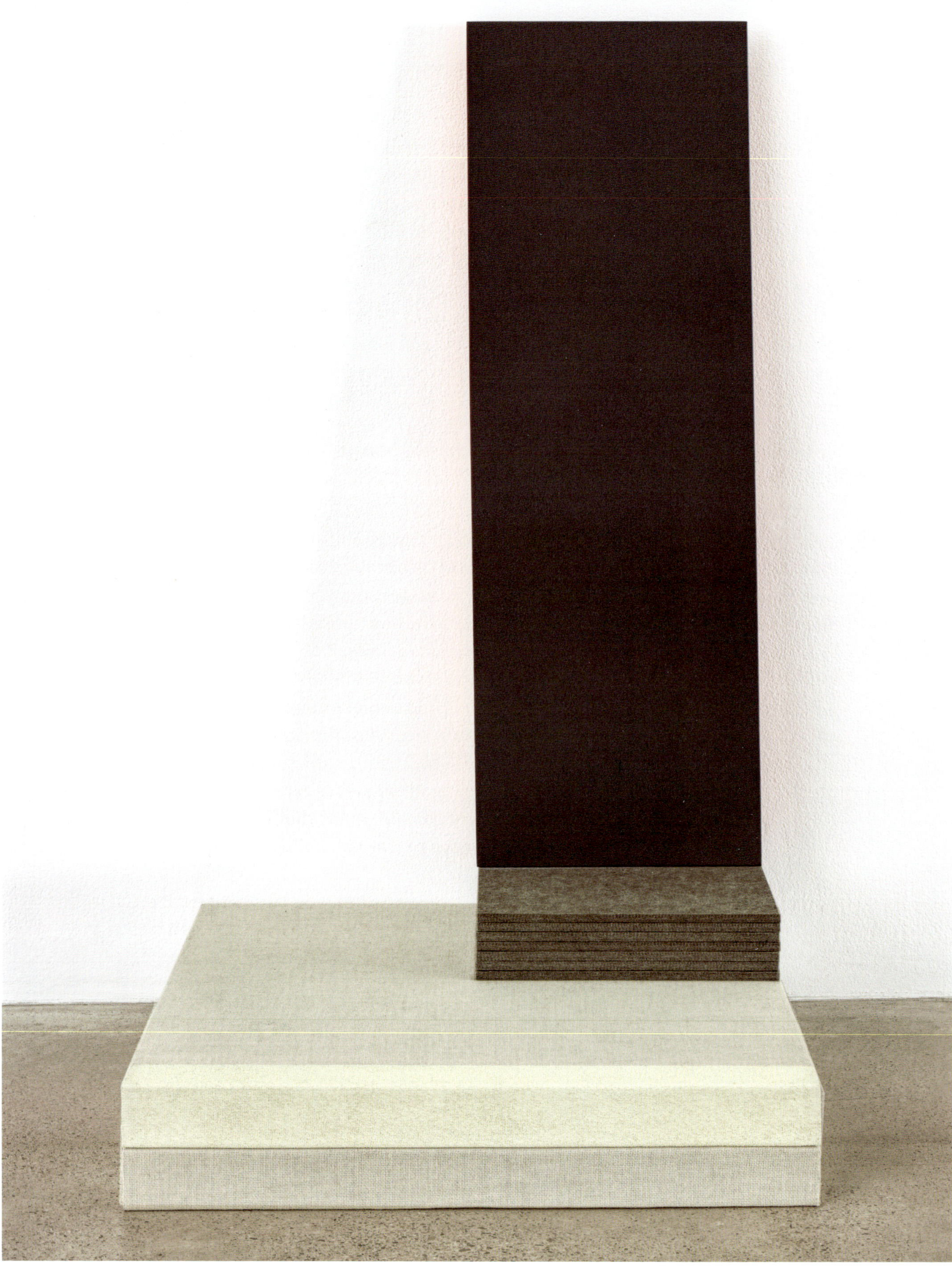

Jennie C. Jones, *Long Low Rest with Hum***, 2025**

Acrylic, acoustic panel, and architectural felt on canvas, 49⅝ × 48 × 3½ inches (126 × 121.9 × 8.9 cm)

 Courtesy Alexander Gray Associates, New York

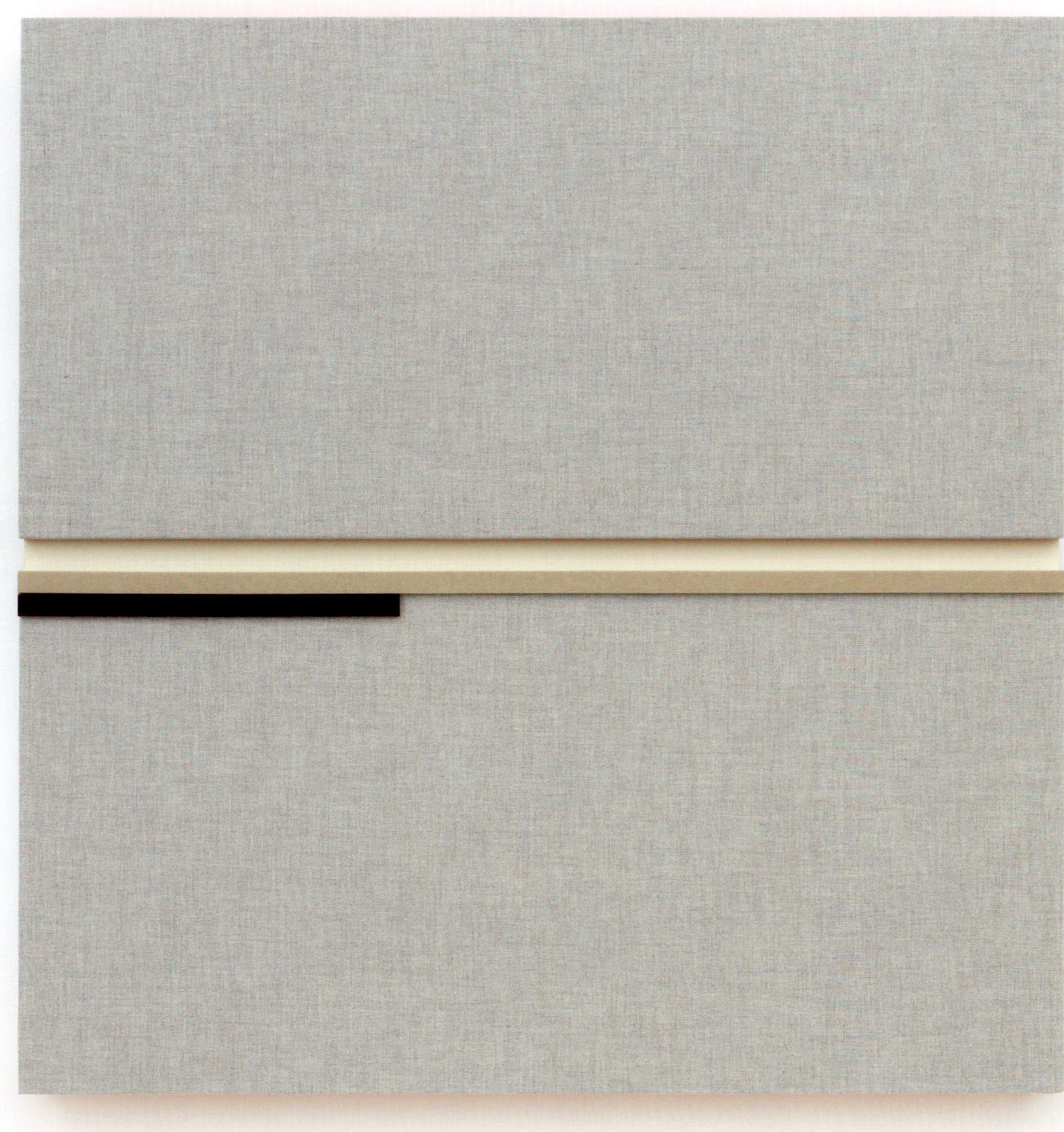

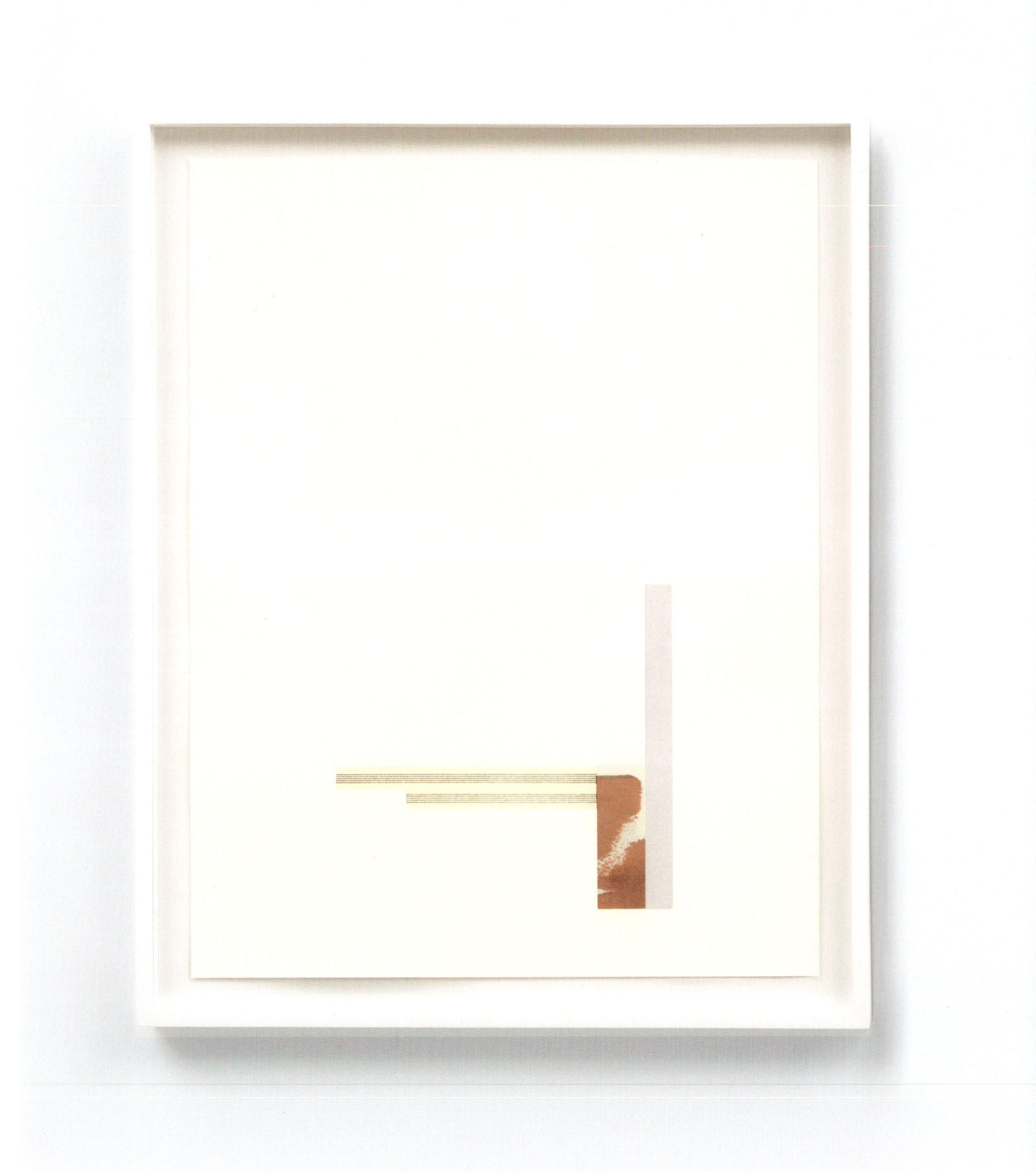

Jennie C. Jones, *Complex Octaves Diptych #1,* **2025**
Acrylic on paper in 2 parts, 25¾ × 19¾ inches (65.4 × 50.2 cm) each
Courtesy Alexander Gray Associates, New York

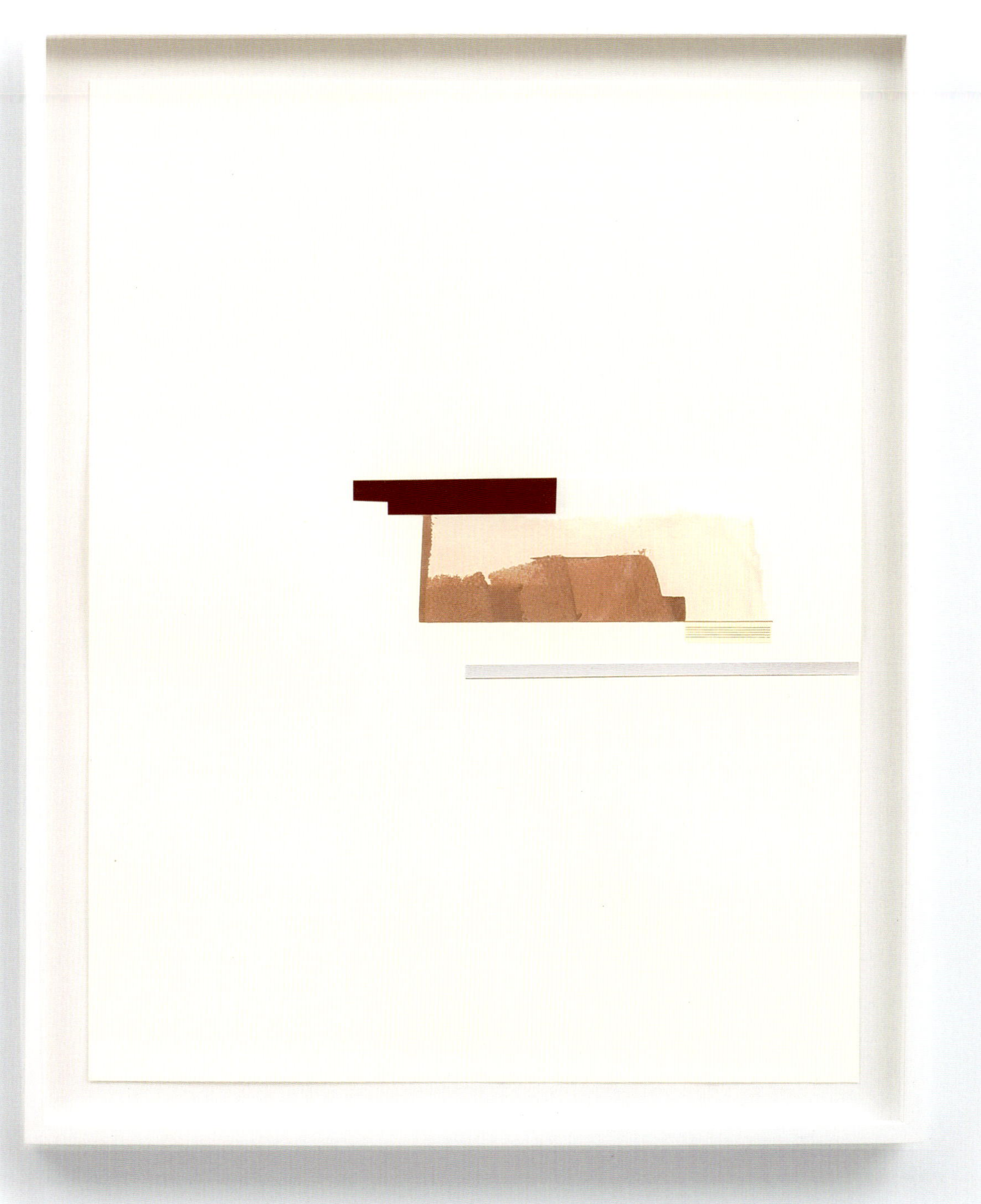

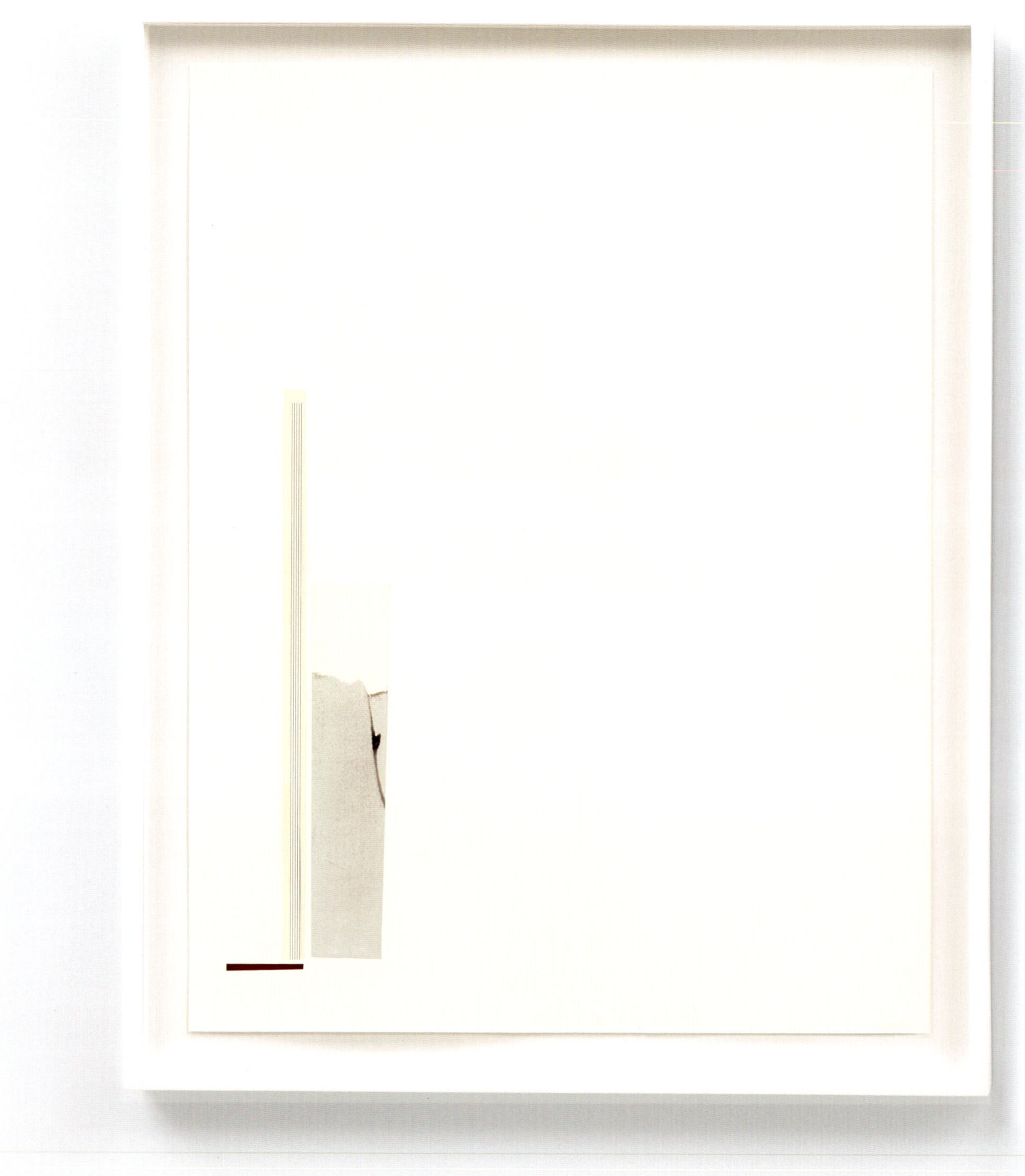

Jennie C. Jones, *Complex Octaves Diptych #2*, 2025
Acrylic on paper in 2 parts, 25¾ × 19¾ inches (65.4 × 50.2 cm) each
Courtesy Alexander Gray Associates, New York

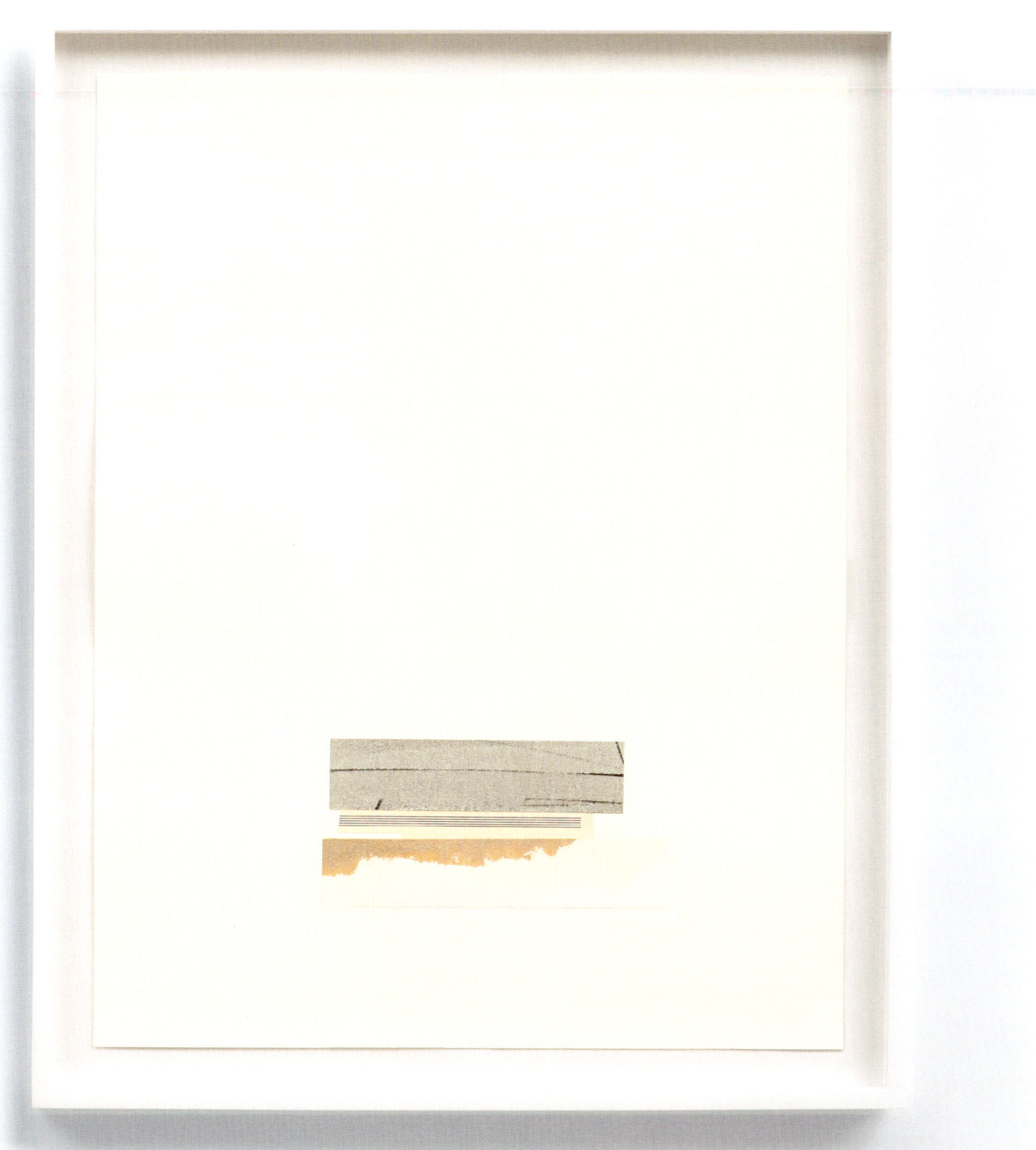

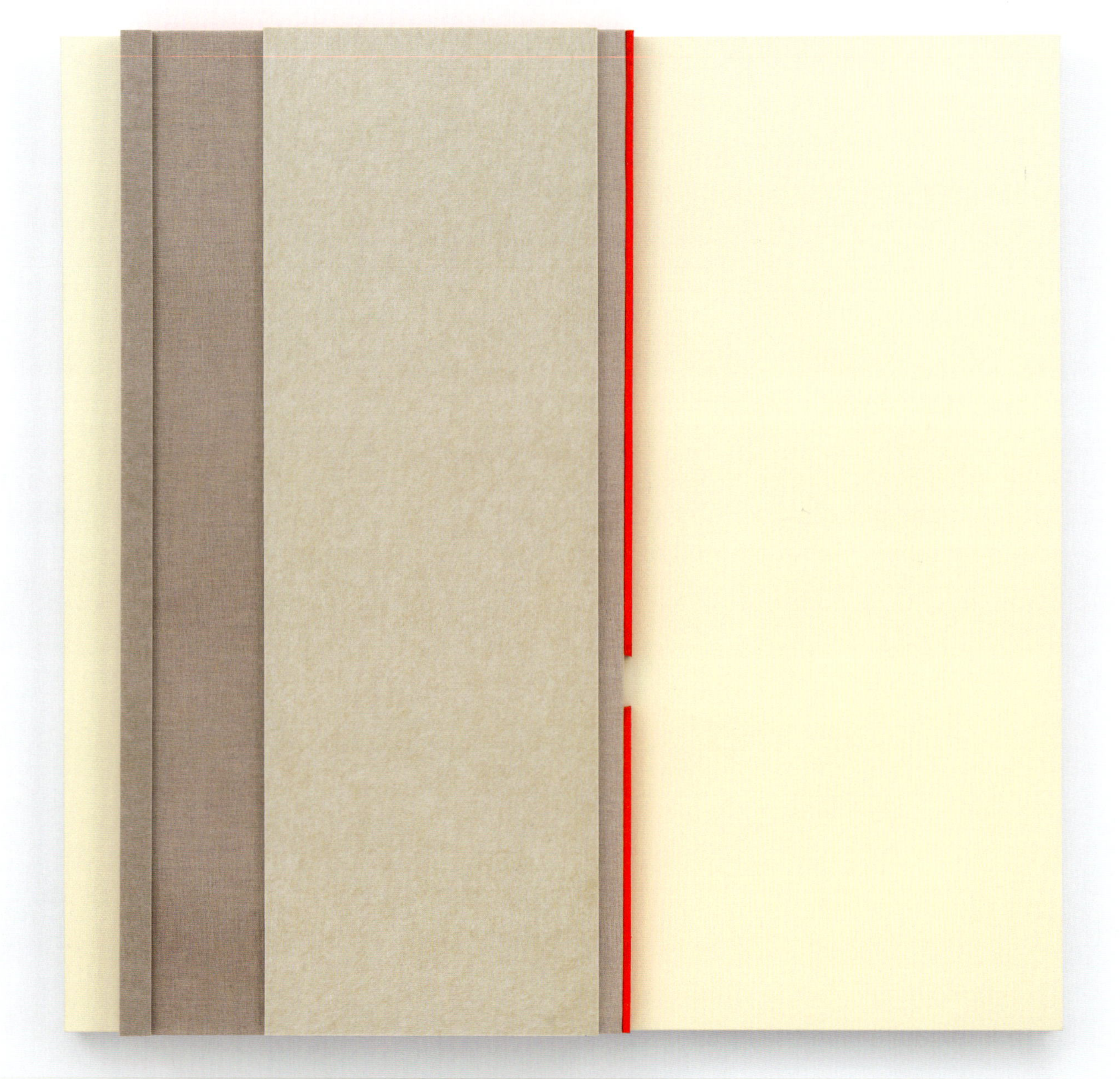

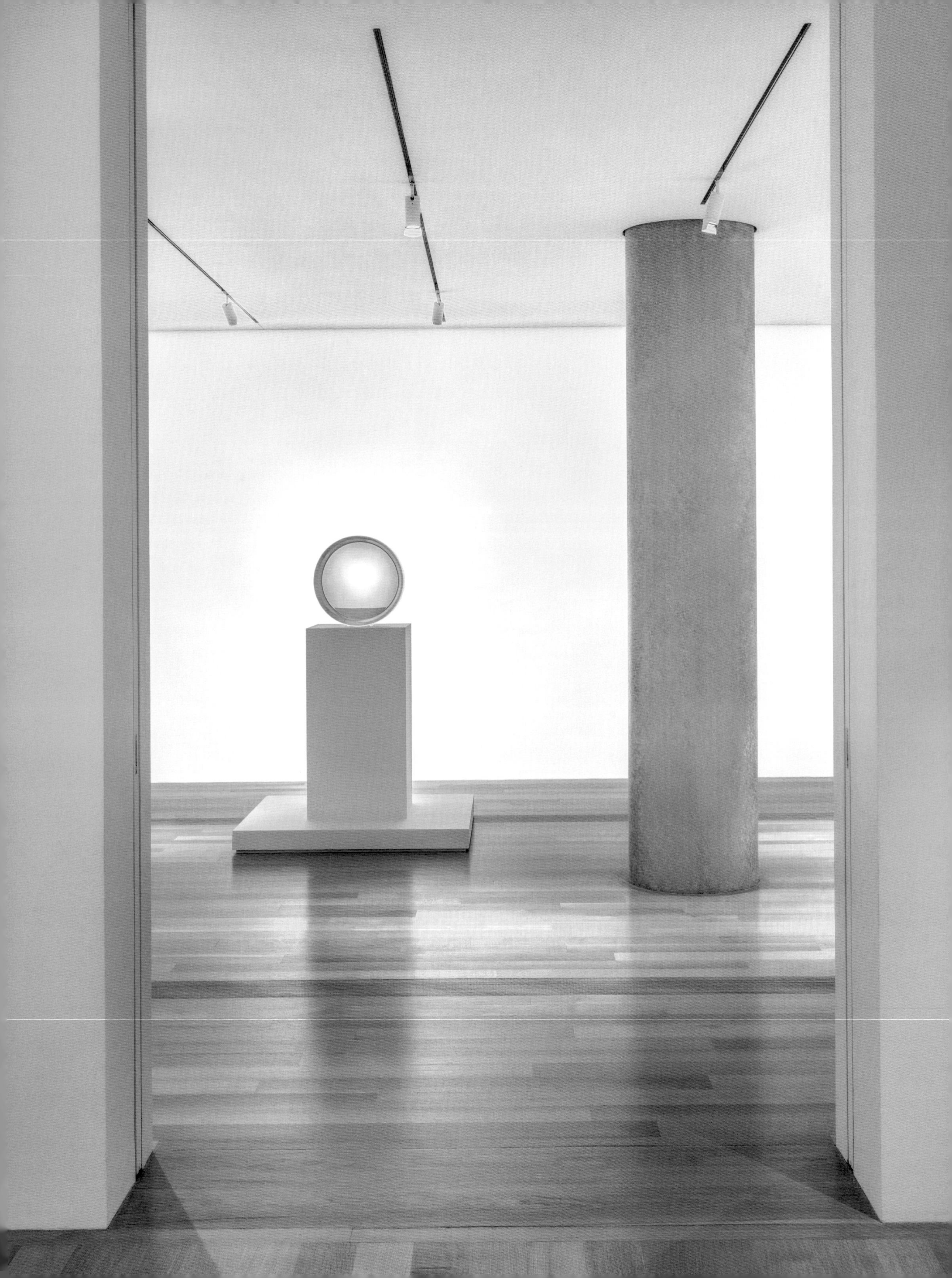

OTHER OCTAVES

JENNIE C. JONES

Expand on the initial text from this notebook after the site visit—but don't let the catalogue essay become bloated with justifications. Don't tell a story— there's an intuitive logic to it. Don't dismiss the pleasure of looking, of loving, respecting, and connecting with the selected artworks.

A curator once used the term "loose hang" to describe an installation of objects in a way that gives space and breadth between artworks when considering their placement. This is the concept that shaped this group exhibition, *Other Octaves.* This is my first foray into organizing an exhibition. At the core of the artists gathered here is my own internal narrative, one that assumes an unfathomable kindred spirit between them—what Fred Eversley once called "energy flux."

There is an unnameable connective tissue between these thoughtfully selected artists—maybe that thread is found through their commitment, tenacity, radicality—a pushing against or continuing on with the work, chasing the thing. Most works are a product of their time or, conversely, a turning away from the trends of their time. In sonic terms, leave the lure of melody and embrace the dissonant. This gathering of unintentional allies stretches into the realm I refer to as "other octaves."

This linkage is not overt; maybe it is. Perhaps through the use of systems, color found in their gardens or scores, forms, patterns, math, notes, and an awareness of time. I began by seeking hard edges, soft touches, followed by monochromes, precise pencil lines, numeric self-soothing, and focused attention—each a way of holding the present.

This congregation is a deeply personal indulgence—corralled from the spark-plug corner of my mind. A line when broken begins again, a picking up of the gauntlet, but not, more the gesture of dropping it all together. Something also here addresses an aesthetics of absence, occasionally punctured by noise or color.

"Begins again" is the prompt to "Stay on it," as Julius Eastman expresses in his score of the same title. His opening lyrics, not spoken in any performance of the score I've been able to find, read as such:

Change this thread on which we move
from invisible to hardly tangible …
ties that move and break,
disappear, and return again, are not ties
that stay on it.
They are sometimy bonds.

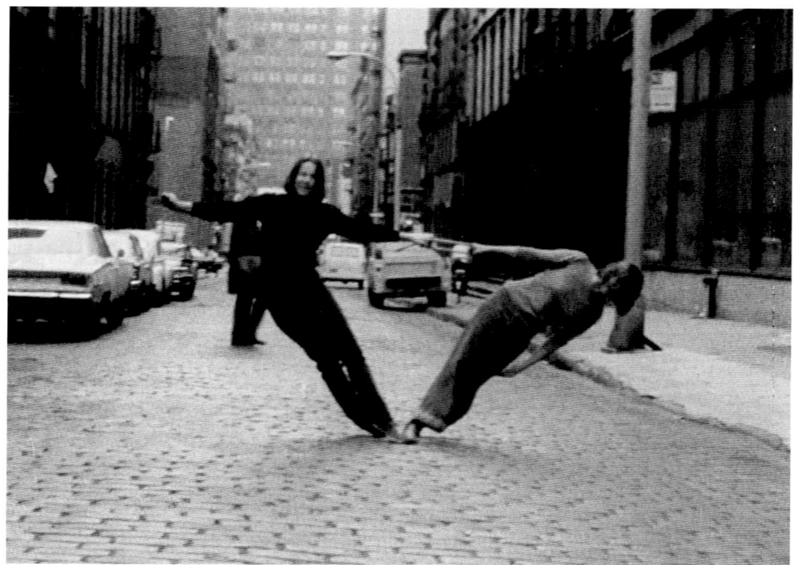

Fig. 1. Trisha Brown, still from *Leaning Duets*, 1970, 16mm film transferred to high-definition video (black and white, silent), 2:21 min., photograph. The Museum of Modern Art, acquired in part through the generosity of the Robert Rauschenberg Foundation, Sarah Arison, Jody & John Arnhold, and Agnes Gund, 69.2019

To that end I say clearly, proximity does not make for equations; group showings are not meant to be equalizing gestures. Standing next to someone isn't standing in the same place or even time. I've seen artists curate themselves into a dreamscape, trying to slip into an equal footing. Not my intention here. I indulge my younger art school self—gobsmacked and humble. Call like a dinner bell to the table those that have been pure inspiration.

There is effort here in this Ando space, an effort in the attempt—like Trisha Brown's *Leaning Duets* (fig. 1).[1] The stacked linearity of the Pulitzers' Tadao Ando–designed building creates a dance from the lower level gallery of selected artists to my own work. It becomes performative in a way, a gesture of moving through struggle, through pedagogy, a "sometimy" bond.

There's an honest, elegant attempt in all the works—fragile, serious, beautiful. Attempt and effort reside here, in this gathering. So much of it feels like a necessary reminder, perhaps more than ever. "Attempting" as a concept in itself is something I've always found compelling. An attempt is somehow different from risk, a first gesture leading to deeper exploration.

To be adjacent over time, beginning again—generatively, in a constant state of woodshedding,[2] inventiveness within the parameters of scale, form, materials, pattern, variation on a theme for eternity. Being the boundary—if one even exists.

It's nearly impossible to write about all of this because, mostly, the visual story says everything. The artist-as-curator offers something through the side door, both better and a potential failure. Perhaps all are only truly tied to each other in material, tone, and my imagination.

1　"Leaning Duets [1], 1970. Five couples, feet together, side of foot touching partner's, leaning out to arm's length, maintaining straight posture. Partners choose a direction, walking in that direction, touching side of foot together with each step. Fallen persons were hauled back up by partner while keeping foot contact. Rope device with handles also employed to achieve greater angle. —Trisha Brown," in *Trisha Brown: Dance and Art in Dialogue, 1961–2001*, ed. Hendel Teicher (Addison Gallery of American Art, Phillips Academy, 2002), 306.

2　"'Woodshedding,' or shedding, is a term commonly used to describe the act of practicing some endeavor, usually in private, to improve one's proficiency in performing it. It is typically used by musicians to mean rehearsing a difficult passage repeatedly, until it can be performed flawlessly." Wikipedia, "Woodshedding," last modified March 22, 2025, at 15:44 (UTC), https://en.wikipedia.org/wiki/Woodshedding.

Fig. 2. Anne Truitt, *Sound Nine*, 2003. Acrylic on paper, 19½ × 19½ inches (49.5 × 49.5 cm). Collection of Steve Elmendorf

Anne Truitt

The title of my MFA thesis exhibition in 1996 was *She Stands*. It was a prideful title at a time of palpable insecurity. I recall this now, in perfect reference to the work of Anne Truitt.

I came to know her work and writing later, far out of school, on my own. She came to discover her sonic conceptual interest later in her practice. Truitt's *Sound* series was created in 2003, one year before her death at age eighty-three. In a letter written to her daughter, referencing this body of work, she writes: "Certain ways in which I have made my work ever since 1961 have simply—very simply, silently and without saying goodbye—departed from me.…Yesterday while walking around, it occurred to me that the "name" of the things I am making out of the beautiful delicate strong paper…is SOUND." Sound—whether perceived as a vibration, a texture, the source of sorrow or jubilation, a disruption, or a lullaby—is something I've been considering in relation to visual art for nearly thirty years.

My hesitation, my complex relationship with color, is real. It has become its own investigation. This ongoing exploration deepens a connection to Truitt's work—there is comfort, even safety, in being transfixed by limiting the palette or embracing neutral tones like in *Sound Nine* (fig. 2). The tender power of *Harvest Shade* (page 77), a sculpture that coincided with my own deeply personal return to yellow hues, holds this energy.

Close looking, close listening, might reveal a brushstroke, the mark of the hand. How daring for that to interrupt form, surface, and shape—yet still hold a presence; both paper and sculpture remain what they are independently.

In the quietude of Truitt's work, there is a restrained energy, a dialogue between form and silence. It is a testament to an elegant stillness, a resonant meditation where color and geometry exist not to fill space but to reveal it. Truitt's forms, delicately poised, invite us to perceive the subtle vibrations between perception, reality, and time.

Anne activated color into form and, eventually, into sound.

She Stands.

Free Thoughts on a Convening of Artists:

Common ground is nothing more
than finger-tip touch of a maker,

from immaterial to material

breathing all the spaces in between
while
sunlight crawls across the studio floor
the only tracing of hours

tone, color, a mutual logic
approach—a yearning

fields and edges
fields of green
The lure of green in this context
becomes symbolic of proliferation

an outgrowth like moss,
reactivated
with the misting of water—
spreading it shifts into pinks and yellows
and dusk and dawn, coda
pollination

Paper

A low-risk material,
fast but tender, precise
or slow, or tossed in the bin
pages or drawings
books or scores
that are transmitted
heard, in one's interior voice or
sung, sing, tap
instructional or interpretative

A Red Tree in High Winter

To be forgotten, sometimes remembered,
revised, re-contextualized
artworks in shadow box storage
then in white box light, again,
time traveling like all objects
having the same, exact, conversations

To be forgotten, sometimes remembered,
a conceptual visitation—amidst the scrolling no less
or some such reference to how history slips past us now,
on small screens
brief meaning or an entire lifespan,
becomes reduced to an elliptical motion,
to brush against surface with ink or paint,
a different kind of light touch
more adjacent over time

What do a few selected titles read like as a list, song, poem?

Quiet Movement

String Music
Wood Picture
Harvest Shade
Green Form
Blanco y Verde
Sound Nine
Pavanne (Green)
Month III (March)
Métissage (Camouflage)
Wall
Spring Dryad
Nine Part Black Theme
A Communication Village

Benevolence

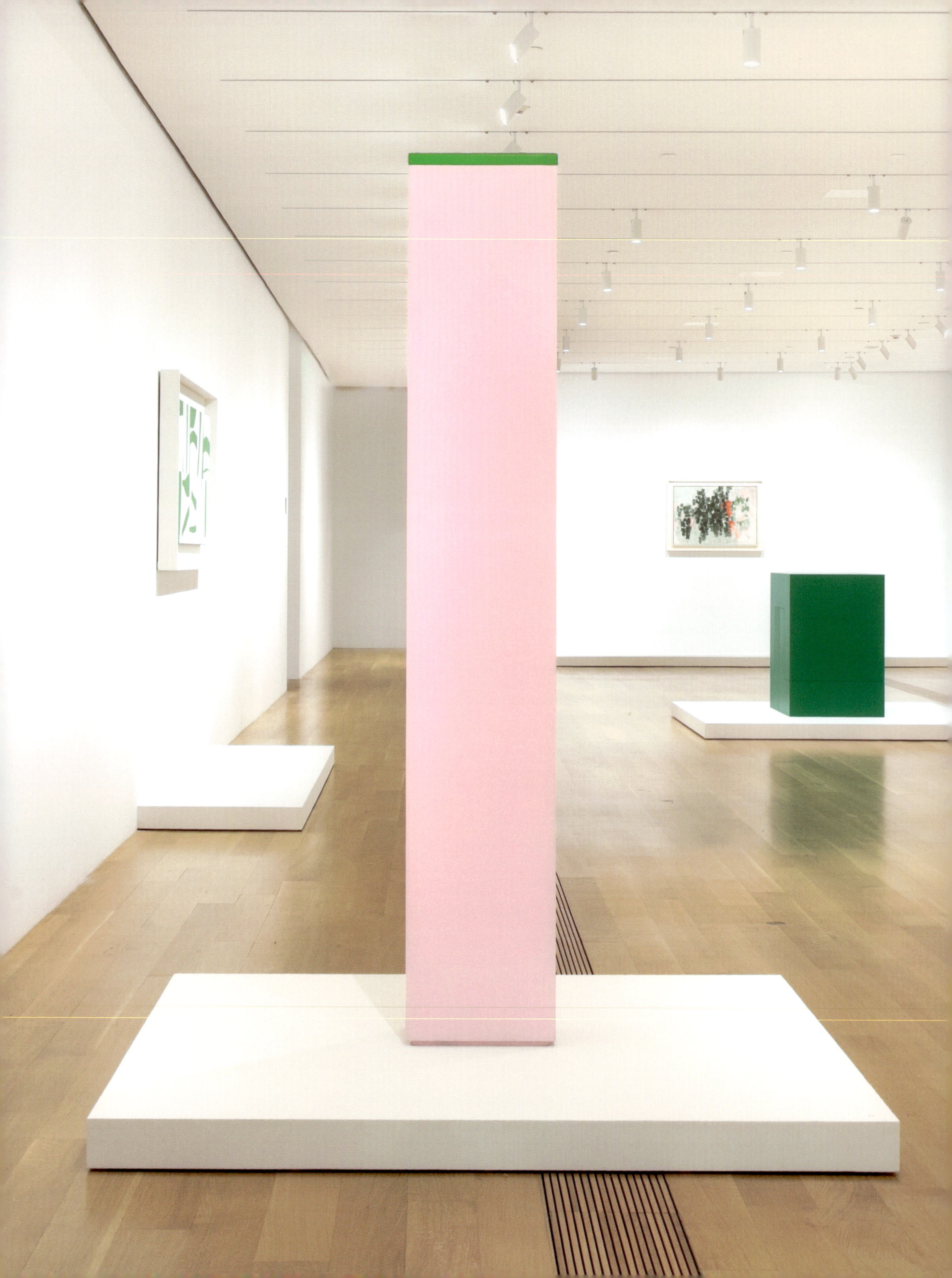

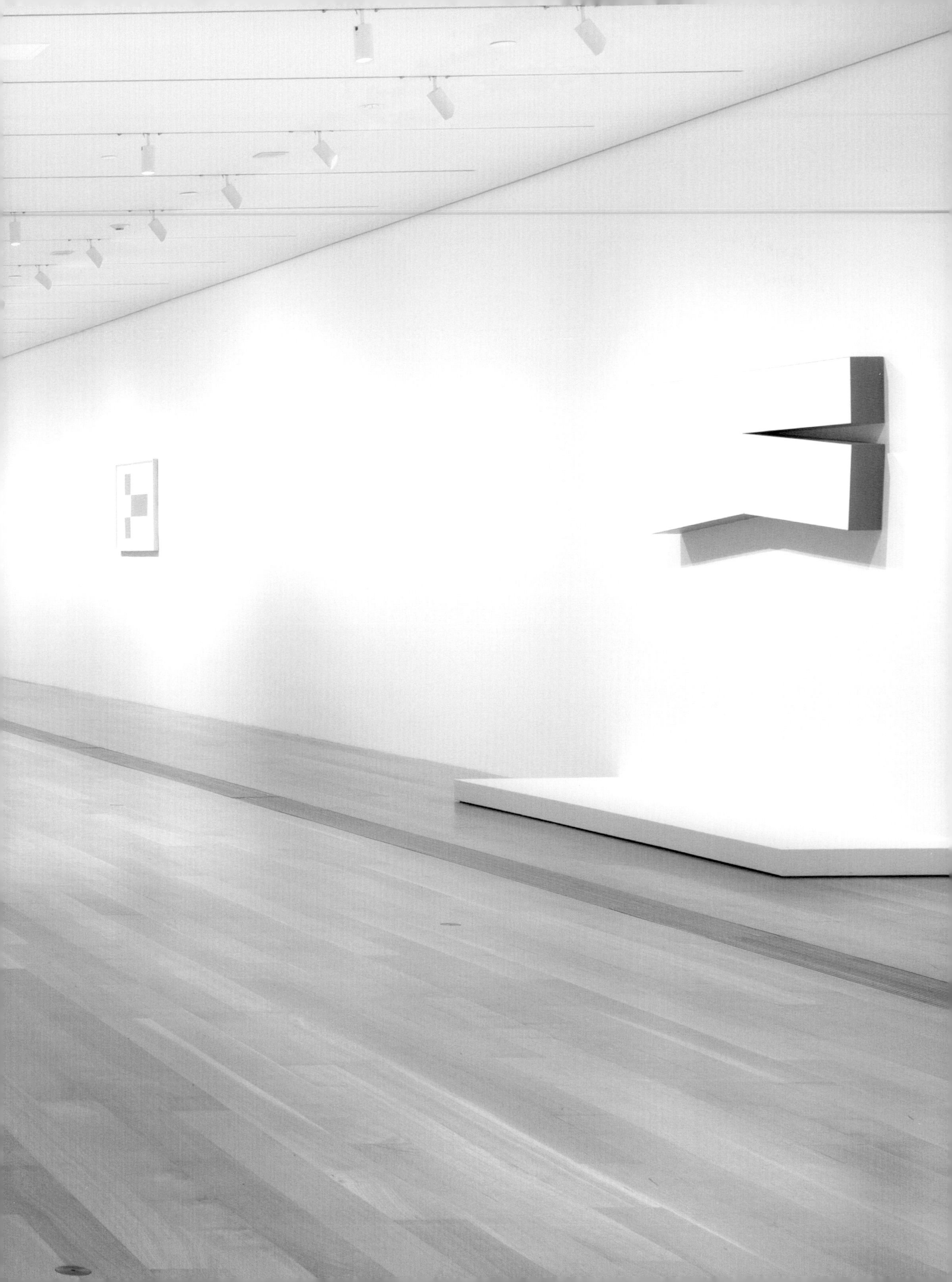

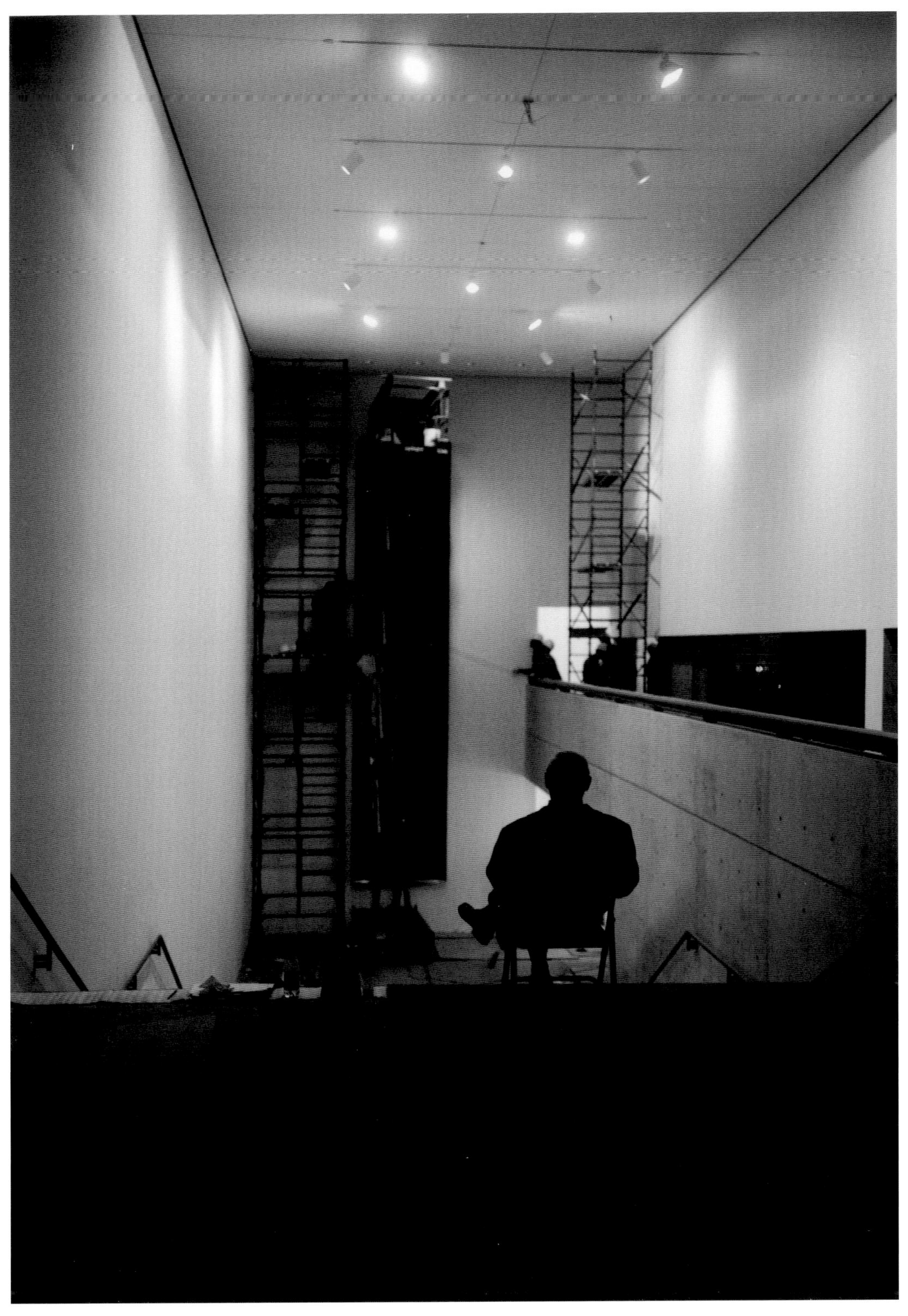

Ellsworth Kelly supervising the installation of *Blue Black*, The Pulitzer Foundation for the Arts, St. Louis, 2001. Jack Shear, courtesy Ellsworth Kelly Studio

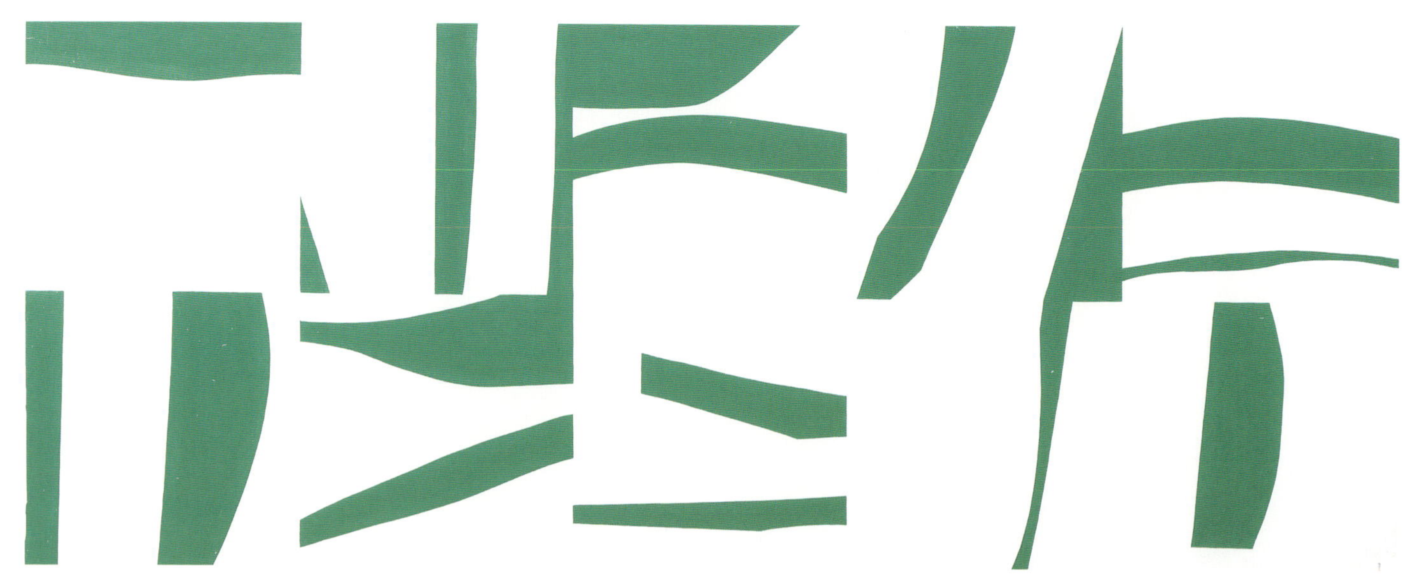

Ellsworth Kelly, *Talmont***, 1951**

Oil on canvas, 26 × 64½ inches (66 × 163.8 cm)
Collection of Jack Shear

JENNIE C. JONES

Blue

Fourteen days after I autographed a copy of my first monograph as a gift to be given to Ellsworth Kelly, he died, at the age of 92. He lived a long well-spent life, painting. I had complicated feelings about him—a mixture of love, disdain, admiration, and envy.[1]

When I was a student at the Art Institute of Chicago in the late 1980s, the school began installing a large suite of Kelly paintings, displacing several other artists' works and filling the entire mezzanine balcony space of the museum. I had a hard time with them. The air then was thick with sociopolitical issues and changes—the culture wars were on. I was twenty, immersed in the new multicultural ferment.[2]

In hindsight, my distress over Kelly was mostly about the politics of the moment, the push for inclusion in the canon and the scholarly struggle against white patriarchal authority. I was angry at his freedom! I wanted to effect change, but I also wanted to be that unrestricted, free to meditate on form, to look at the color of a blue jay's cap or the rounded red belly of a fat robin and see the curve as a composition. I was, after all, a girl from Ohio whose first drawings were of trees.

I was almost ashamed to like Ellsworth Kelly or Agnes Martin, among others; later, after shaking off the impact of graduate school, I made it my mission to investigate my then secret Minimalist leanings. I was not ashamed to like Ornette Coleman, whom we also lost in 2015. I left painting around 2000, and during a long sojourn replaced it with listening, until I could circle back years later, like the curve of the robin's belly, right into the arch of the Hirshhorn Museum.[3]

In December 2015, opening my mid-career survey at the Contemporary Arts Museum Houston, I signed a catalogue with shaky hands: *For Ellsworth, my hero, thank you.*

Turning

The introduction of the Harmon Foundation awards in 1926, which were always dispensed with a flurry of publicity, marked the beginning of a new era for Negro visual art. With its private endowment, popular social mission, and interracial alliances, [the

*institution] possessed a much greater public relations capacity
than any prior initiatives.... Due in large part to the activities
of the Harmon Foundation, African Americans emerged as a distinct
presence in the American art world.*[4]

I contend that, with the best of intentions, the William E. Harmon Foundation established a set of formally conservative aesthetic guidelines for both content and method, which we are still grappling with today.[5] I consistently ask myself, what is my intention? Who is my audience? Where does my truth lie and what is my role as a "cultural producer," regardless of reward, within a broken, market-driven system.

Sam Gilliam, Jack Whitten, Stanley Whitney, and Martin Puryear, although not quite all the same generation, are in vogue again, proudly displaying their gray hairs from years of pure devotion, tenacity, skill, and commitment to their practice. Alma Thomas recently hung again at the Whitney Museum, where she had a one-woman show back in 1972. I'm sure that because of my preoccupation with making art, while not keeping up with critical texts, nothing I'm presenting here is surprising. I am aware that there is a lot more to unpack. Is this a rant? Or am I turning, face forward, to delve into Kelly's liberty? Why was I not introduced to these African American artist-heroes alongside Ellsworth in 1989?

Gray

I leap from the whirlpool of the binary and say, my blackness is not that of a Malevich, Newman, Reinhardt, or the like; it is mine. Leaving behind a reductive pigment-based curation or a simplistic reframing of "black painting" as my signifying monkey—I ponder Gray. Not as a color of watered-down blackness, of neutrality reflecting a weakness of stance—it is, after all, the color of concrete. Gray is a reflection of multiplicity, of the anti-essentialist times we currently occupy, where various modes of expression by African American artists are beginning to be embraced.

At my artist's talk on Agnes Martin last fall at the Dia Foundation in New York, I read the following page from my sketchbook, a "musing" written in soft pencil:

*Gray, a color, non color all colors mixed together with a drop
of light to make it comforting, easy. It's "clean" yet the color
of dust. Soft yet the color of cement, steel, lead, or graphite—
simultaneously a fluffy cloud, pregnant with the possibility of
rainwater. There is generosity in that gray sky—away from the
harshness of the binary. Generosity in the quiet overcast days*

when those sun worshipers, my harsh enemies, go indoors. In that
quiet, I can draw and listen and feel at ease.

Over You

Jazz, my love; since Ken Burns gave you
a capital "J"
    I want to rename you.
Since Wynton stays on the "A" train, I
want to jump
    the tracks, be derailed.
Since you exemplify my very interest in
the sonic,

I want to call you my bitch.
Since you still keep me captive, while
you are the
    one with Stockholm syndrome,
I'm just going to take you slowly into
my hands and
    be present.

Originally printed in Art in America, *March 2016, 54-55.*

1   "Blue Turning Gray Over You" is the title of a song composed in 1929 by Thomas "Fats" Waller with lyrics by Andy Razaf. Recorded by Billie Holiday, Louis Armstrong, and others, it is considered a jazz standard and a part of the Great American Songbook.

2   My undergraduate years (1987–91) saw protests against the work of Andres Serrano and Robert Mapplethorpe, raising defunding concerns for the NEA, as well as Lucy Lippard's lecture at the School of the Art Institute of Chicago on her book *Mixed Blessings: New Art in a Multicultural America*. The first exhibition of artworks by the student group Artists of Color United (ACU) took place, and bomb threats were made over Dread Scott's installation *What Is the Proper Way to Display a U.S. Flag?* The Guerrilla Girls continued to have critical impact, and the Persian Gulf War played out.

3   My first solo museum exhibition, *Higher Resonance*, curated by Evelyn Hankins, opened at the Hirshhorn Museum and Sculpture Garden, Washington, DC, in 2013.

4   Mary Ann Calo, *Distinction and Denial: Race, Nation, and the Critical Construction of the African American Artist, 1920-40* (University of Michigan Press, 2007), 75.

5   The William E. Harmon Foundation was established in 1922, initially to build playgrounds and provide scholarships in Black communities. It soon became an essential funding source for African American artists, writers, and critics—many of them key figures of the Harlem Renaissance. The Harmon Foundation closed its doors in 1967.

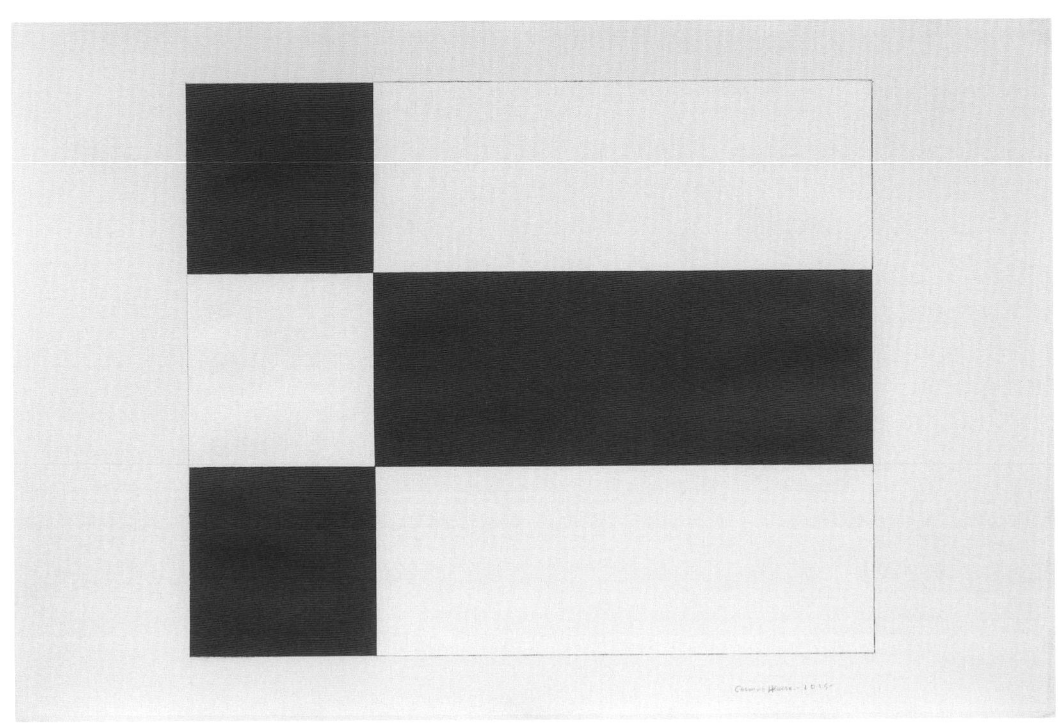

Carmen Herrera, *Untitled*, 2015

Acrylic and pencil on paper, 24½ × 36½ inches (62.2 × 92.7 cm)

 Courtesy of Lisson Gallery

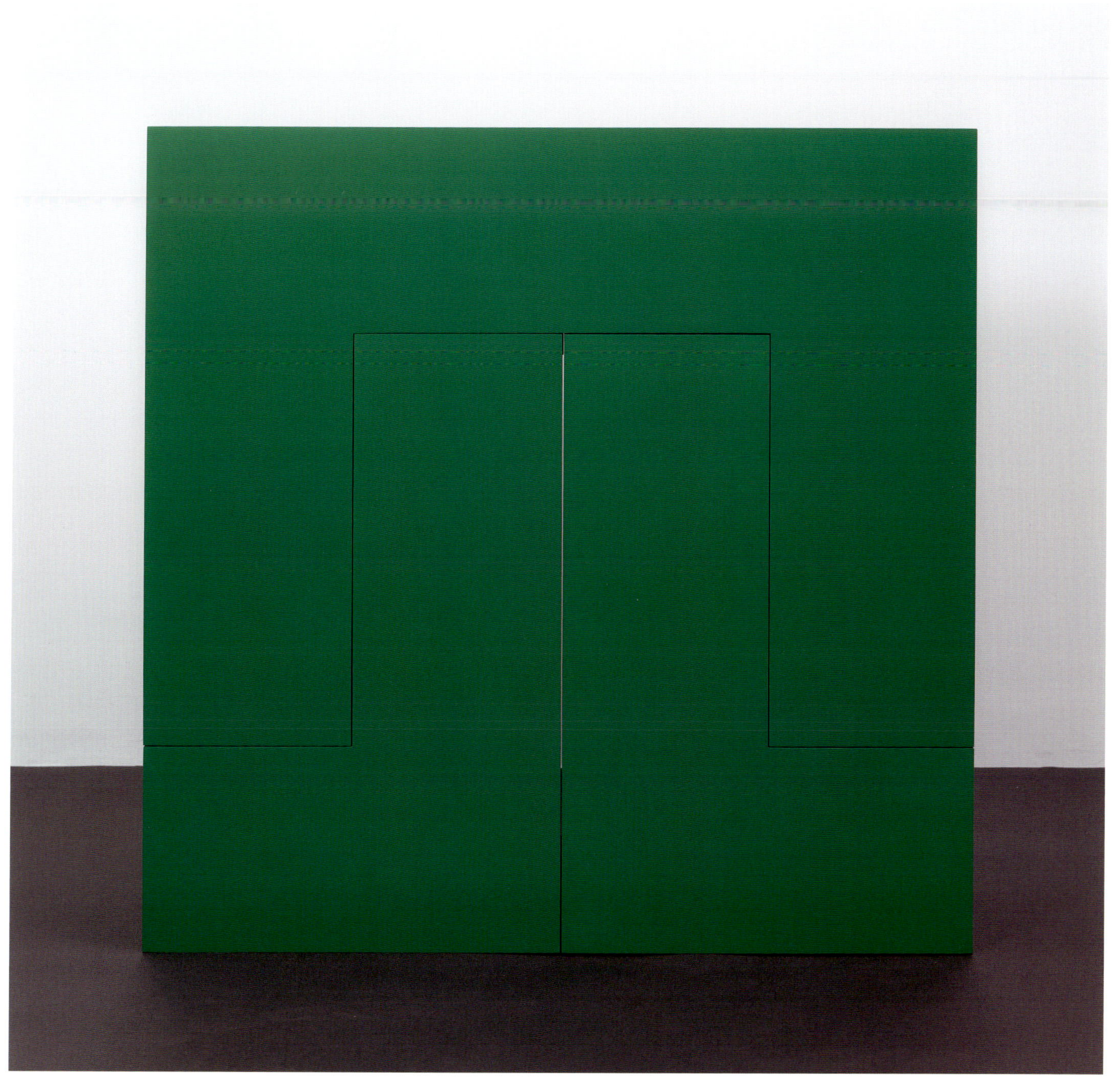

Carmen Herrera, *Pavanne (Green)*, 1967/2016
Acrylic and aluminum, 35⅞ × 35⅞ × 23⅞ inches (91.1 × 91.1 × 60.6 cm)
Courtesy of Lisson Gallery

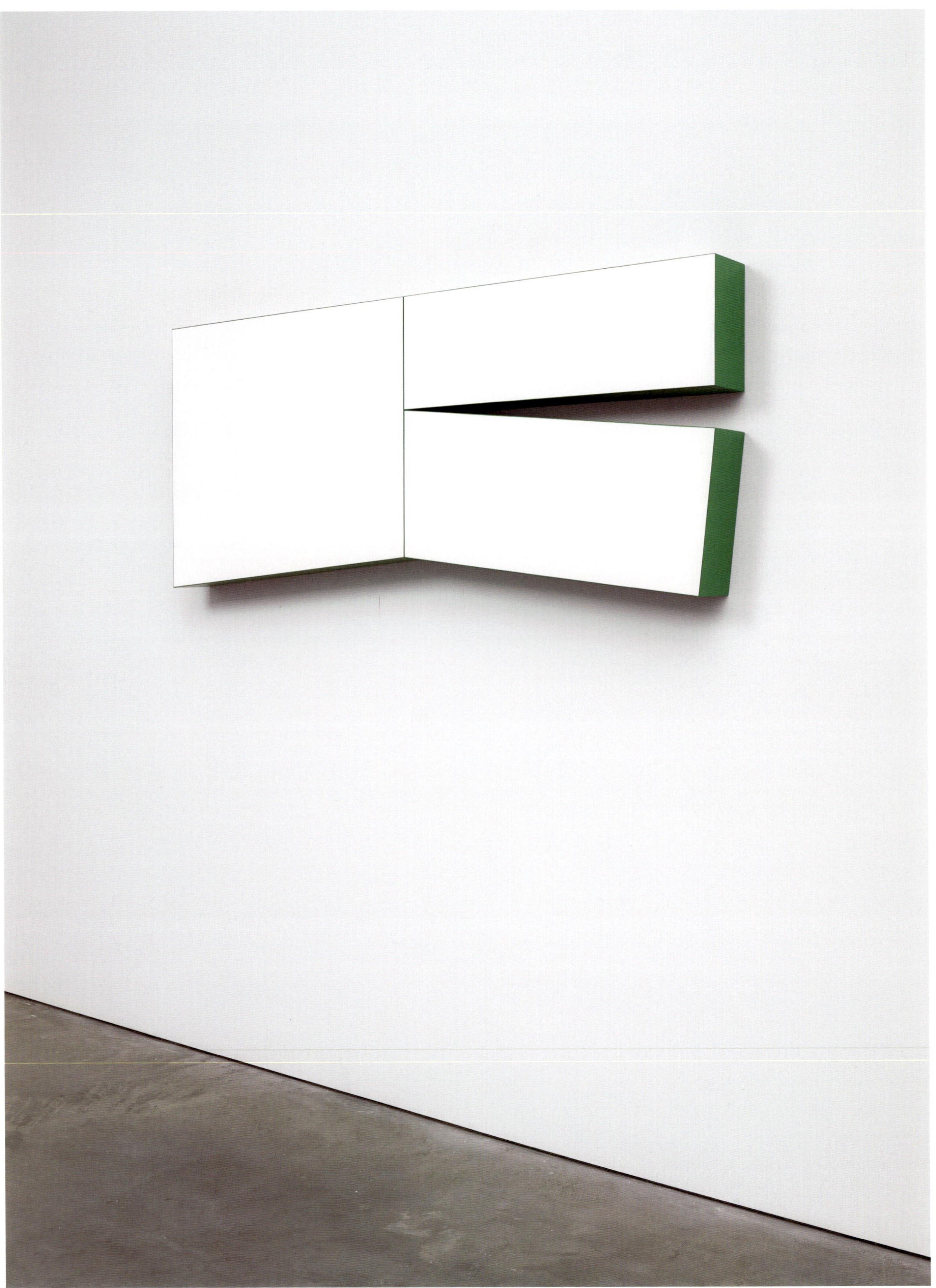

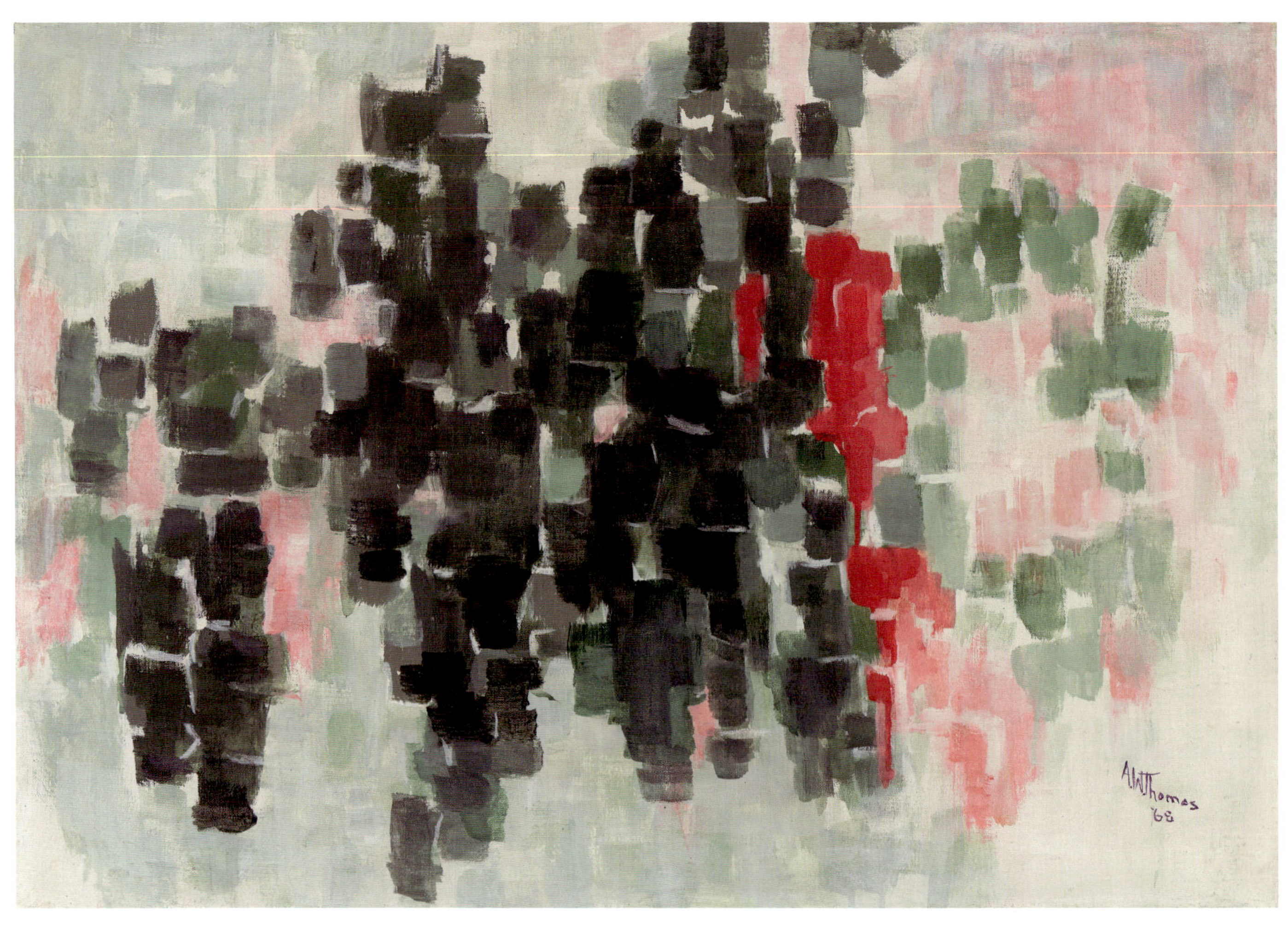

Alma Thomas, *Red Tree in High Winter*, 1968
Acrylic and graphite on canvas, 24 × 34¼ inches (61 × 87 cm)
Colby College Museum of Art, Waterville, Maine. Museum purchase from the Jere Abbott Acquisitions Fund

JENNIE C. JONES

Syntax

The repetition in Alma Thomas's work suggests, to me, the tenacity of her language. When encountering her paintings, I am struck by their transformative nature, each stroke a word, words building towards a sentence, sentences to paragraphs—her vision is one that translates the beauty of the world back to us, encompassing the grandness of cosmic systems to the small details of flower petals. A gesture that says, "I'm here," over and over again. We see this most clearly in her later painting *Starry Night and the Astronauts* (1972). Like other works from this period, including *Apollo 12 "Splash Down"* (1970), *Starry Night* pays homage to humankind's existential quest, our desire to explore, at the same time that it recognizes and values our accomplishments in this area. Her works seem to be created while in a state of total presence, similar to stargazing, and the mindfulness in her process comforts me. The consistency of her brushstroke, even when she is struggling with arthritis, reveals the pleasure she takes in it. This is a working method that acknowledges the moment in which each brushstroke was made. It is an exhibition that comprises a lifetime of touch. My own aesthetic was formed through my 1970s childhood. Alma's work was also responding to and operating in tandem with movements and art forms such as concrete poetry,[1] quilting's reemergence, Earthworks, and Minimalism. Each form suggests a pared-down, hands-on vision of the world, one filled with promise and joy, amidst much darker sociopolitical shifts. Alma is an artist who embodies that type of pure, optimistic energy. She set a precedent, which is continuously inspiring. I've called attention to her work for many years, as I reach for an understanding of my own creative lineage and artistic pedagogy.

Music and Lyrical Movement

While looking at Alma's work, I often hear musical notes. I think of the pianist Ahmad Jamal, particularly "Autumn Leaves" on the album *Ahmad's Blues* (a fitting parallel for Thomas whose work is also engaged with the natural world). Jamal brings the listener to an anxious internal state, repeating a succession of tension-building notes before bouncing off to the break, and releasing us to a gleeful resolution. Alma's patterns also have a kind of improvisational play within them; the repetition can seem tedious, just before hitting the break, just before you start to see the world as she does—cohesive yet fractured.

Like subtone, her under-painting provides depth for the flickering notes that drift above. Her work directly engages with the micro-macro relationship of all things—that one voice, note, or mark has collective resonance.

A Wide Net

In the negative space of her work there exists a loose, organic grid, a net, which made me recall the following passage, seemingly written for Alma:

> *She pulled in her horizon like a great fish net. Pulled it from around the waist of the world and draped it over her shoulder. So much of life in its meshes! She called in her soul to come and see.*

> —*Zora Neale Hurston,* Their Eyes Were Watching God

Originally printed in Alma Thomas *(The Studio Museum in Harlem; The Frances Young Tang Teaching Museum and Art Gallery at Skidmore College; and DelMonico Books/Prestel, 2016), 147.*

1   Concrete, pattern, or shape poetry is a form in which the graphic arrangement of the words is vital to conveying meaning. It is sometimes referred to as visual poetry, a term that has now developed a distinct definition of its own.

Jennie C. Jones, *Standing and Moving #6*, 2024
Collage and acrylic on paper, 25¾ × 19¾ inches (65.4 × 50.2 cm)
Courtesy Alexander Gray Associates, New York

Jennie C. Jones, *Standing and Moving #1–2,* **2024**
Collage and acrylic on paper, 25¾ × 19¾ inches (65.4 × 50.2 cm) each
Courtesy Alexander Gray Associates, New York

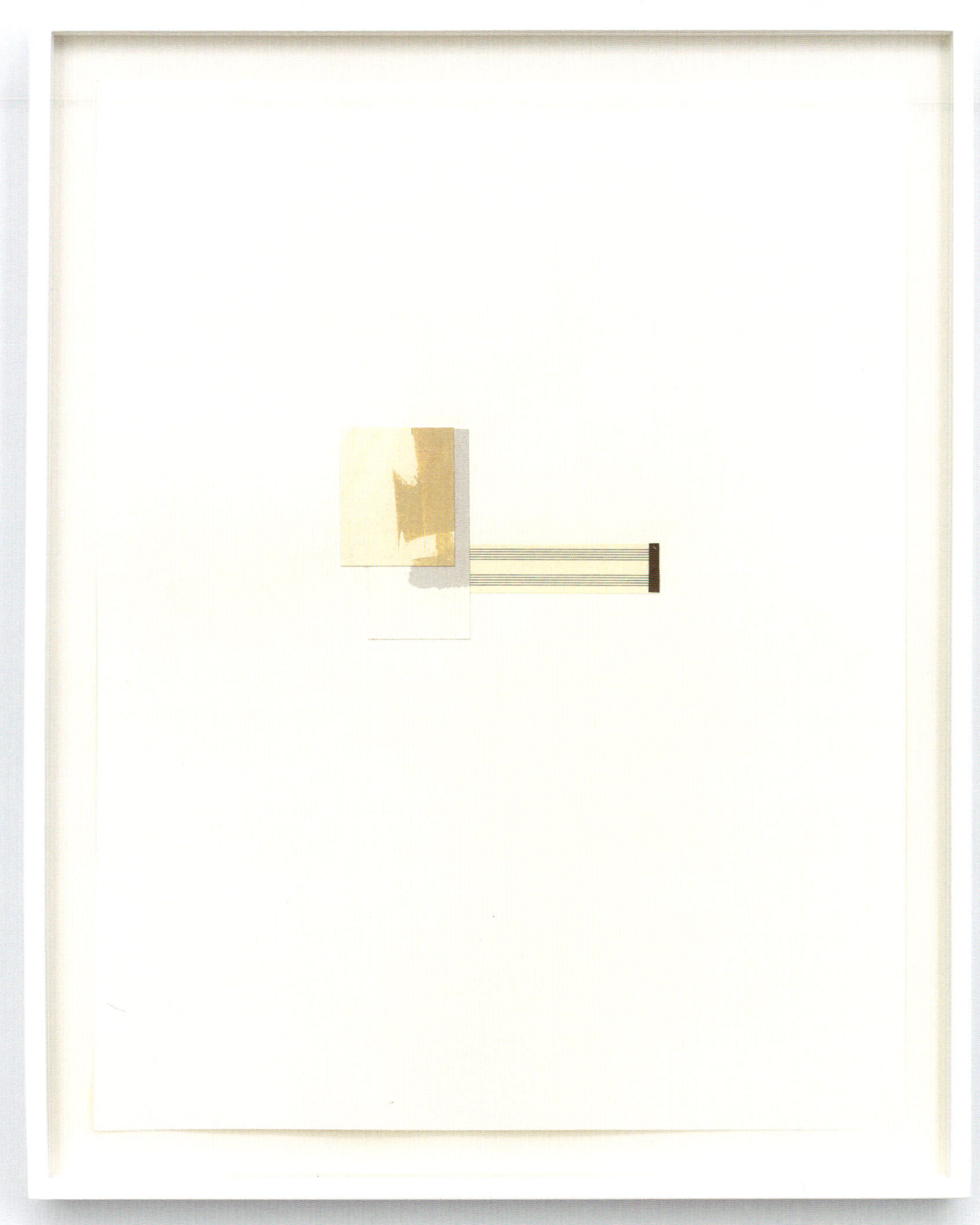

Anne Truitt, *Sound Nine***, 2003**
Acrylic on paper, 19½ × 19½ inches (49.5 × 49.5 cm)
Collection of Steve Elmendorf

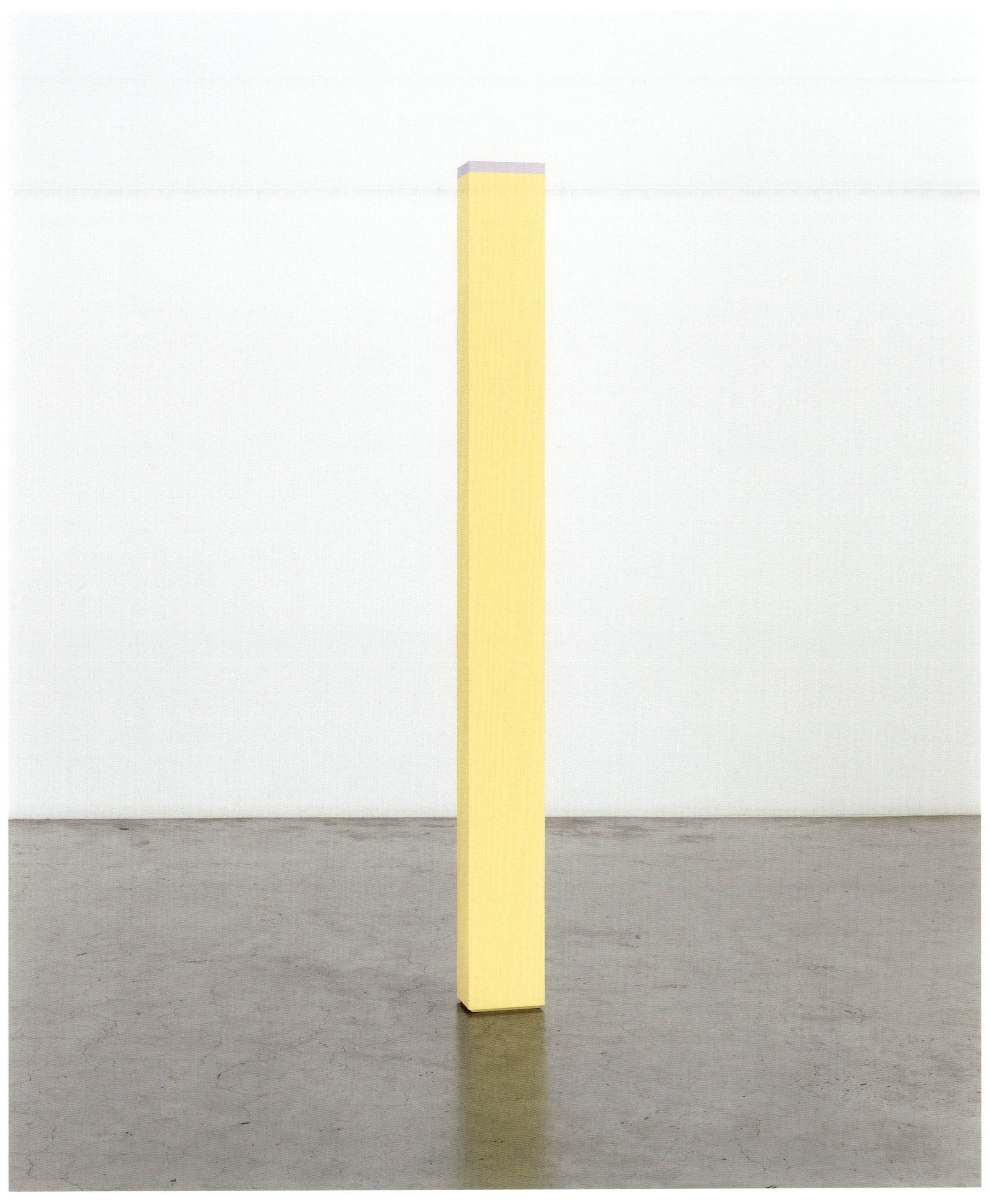

Anne Truitt, *Harvest Shade,* **1996**
Acrylic on wood, 60¼ × 5½ × 4 inches (153 × 14 × 10.2 cm)
Private collection

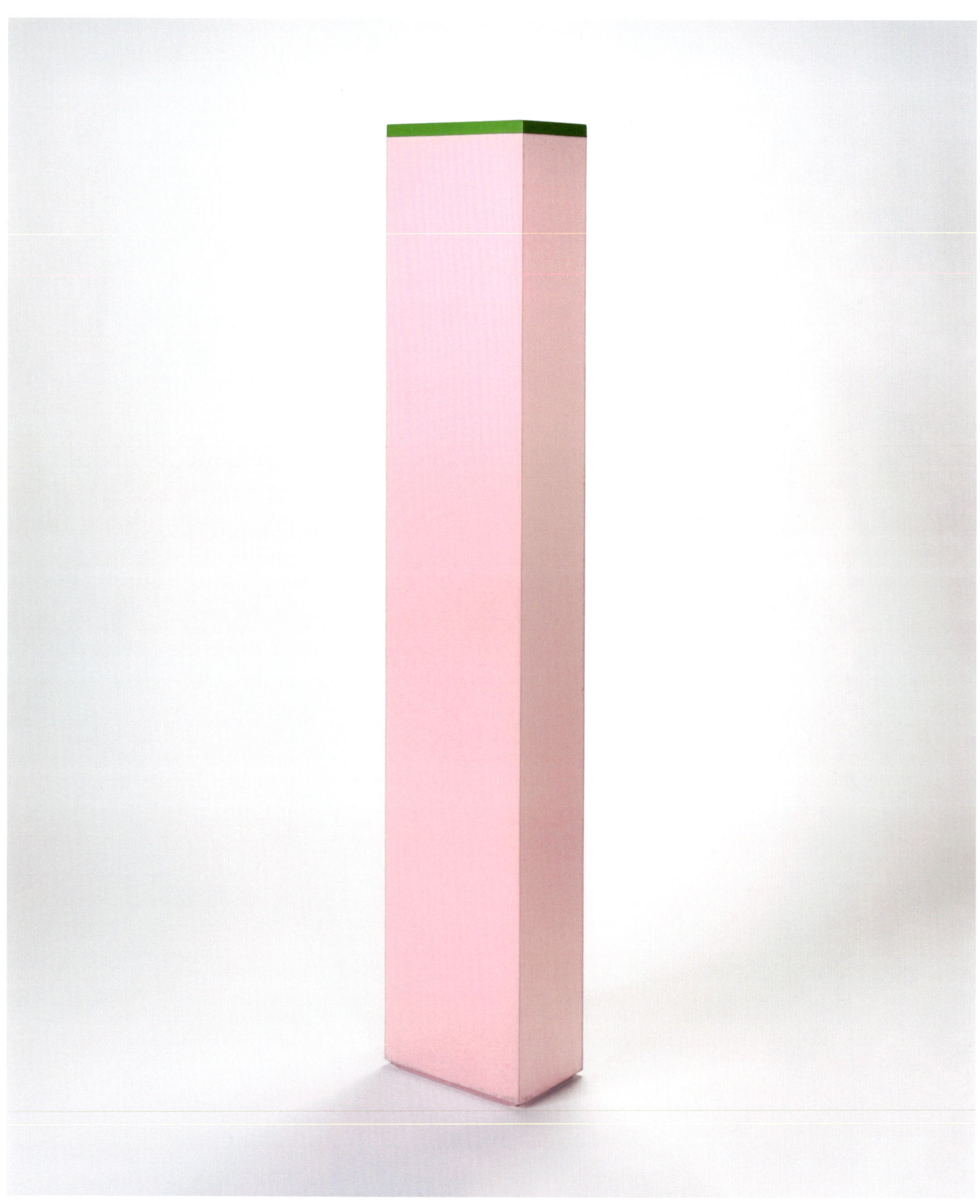

Anne Truitt, *Spring Dryad,* **1975**
Acrylic on wood, 76 × 13 × 8 inches (193 × 33 × 20.3 cm)
Collection of Steve Elmendorf

Anne Truitt, *Sound Fourteen***, 2003**
Acrylic on paper, 19¼ × 19¾ inches (48.9 × 50.2 cm)
Collection of Steve Elmendorf

Agnes Martin, *Benevolence*, 2001

Acrylic and graphite on canvas, 60 × 60 inches (152.4 × 152.4 cm)
Dia Art Foundation; gift of the artist

JENNIE C. JONES

Belief

> Almost everyone believes that art is from the experience of the artist, meaning the intellectually grasped experience. They believe that it is affected by where you live and what you do. But one's "biography," character, abilities, knowledge—all of that has nothing to do with art work. Inspiration is the beginning the middle and the end.... There are no valid thoughts about art. If your sensibilities are awake you will respond.

—Agnes Martin

There is potentially a strong argument against everything that Agnes Martin puts forth in the above statement. It contains an implicit dismissal of multicultural and feminist discourses, as well as the whole of Post-Structuralist theory. It rejects ideas of painting about painting in favor of painting about emotion. However, there is also radical freedom in that statement—there is space, courage, and a refreshing point of view.

Considered one of the most influential Minimalist painters, Martin herself rejected characterizations of her as a Minimalist and self-identified as an Abstract Expressionist. By her account, she was purely and simply expressing her emotions in the work. Her process was to wait for inspiration, to focus on joy, innocence, and love. In my opinion, she had a deep understanding of time, perhaps from a childhood spent among the vast Saskatchewan plains.

Like Martin's belief in inspiration, I believe that unexpected historic junctures spark connection to a greater kind of gladness; pleasure lies in the surprise of commonality all around us. Martin once said that she specifically admired Mark Rothko's work for having "reached for zero, so that nothing could stand in the way of truth."[1]

As an artist, finding associations with another artist's work is deeply personal. Often that connection transcends time, race, and gender, gracefully touching upon some nameless thing that we as creative practitioners are all grasping at. To be blunt, if you are a real artist you are grasping—looking for windows, air, connection, a way to convey something outside of language. Sometimes grasping to fold into the vast lineage of makers, thinkers. Not to a pedagogy or to our specific positionality in the canon, but to our purpose. Maybe a link to an existential thread rather than an obvious existential dread.

The discourse around reductive aesthetics is the often-forgotten sidecar attached to more expressive modes of abstraction. Those expressive, gestural acts, which feed a heroic lineage of artmaking almost to the point of cliché. Particularly when discussing "Black abstraction," others' expectations of that "wildness" is often up for debate. There is an ache inherent in Minimalism—the distillation of so much existential matter into a single line, a solitary gesture. It is an offshoot to a bombastic, expressive discourse around Black abstraction, and it leads to a questioning: What is my Blackness without vigorous expression of my "circumstance"? As an African American woman, Minimalism has felt like a radical path. I consumed and digested the whole of art history to find the will to make a line, to find solace in a deeply personal type of synesthesia. In Martin and in myself I see an austere sense of refusal and of calm control. Like Agnes, I too was once a small girl, looking at the horizon, a blade of grass, the curve of a stick. Ohio, Saskatchewan; same sky, same. Understanding some kind of connection to simplicity, trying to consolidate that expanse of wordlessness into art with

a lowercase "a." For me, writing about her is full of these complexities.

What of art history and the artists I once felt embarrassed to speak of as influential? What of the more complex terrain of the early 1990s, my formative years, when Post-Structuralist theory crashed into "multiculturalism"? Someone once asked me why I admire the work of Agnes Martin. My initial thought was actually a memory of the first time I saw a Rothko painting as ayoung art student at the Art Institute of Chicago in the late 1980s. I wrote in my sketchbook that it was as if he were "tracing the edges of the soul." When I saw a Martin painting, it was like reaching out of myself, beyond the picture plane, but drawing me close at the same time. I was also jealous of both artists' "freedom" and angry at art history, looking for my place in it, ready to rail against it, all because I was and am in love with art and its making.

The cult of personality is strong in the art world. When you add race and gender identity and sexuality and grief and loss, and a childhood full of searching for a voice—it all lands in the world as an art object. Finding a way to pull back the narrative of your life enough to put the work first and foremost is challenging.

Gray/Grey

To gray out, to block out even the noise of our own thoughts, our analytical song sung to our own often obsessive-compulsive thoughts about the

searching—searching for silence. Not like John Cage, but a type of silence that allows for joy to live in the hands, and in that process, focusing on the hand, the mind becomes still. The Bauhaus painter Johannes Itten writes that gray is "mute, but easily excited to thrilling resonances."[2] Infused or juxtaposed with any other color and it transforms itself. You don't expect to find emotion in the gray, but there it is. Beneath the dampness, dishwater, and disappointment, there it is!

I think of gray as a noncolor, all colors mixed together with a drop of light to make it comforting, easy, clean yet the color of dust. Soft yet the color of cement, steel, lead, or graphite. And simultaneously a fluffy cloud, pregnant with the possibility of rainwater. There is love in that gray sky—away from some hard binary—love in the unobtrusive days when those sun worshipers, my harsh enemies, go indoors. When I asked a friend, artist Robert Gober, about the color prior to giving a talk that included his work, he also referenced the sky.

What do I think or feel about gray...? That it interferes with white or blue, but I'm thinking of paint and sky. Someone said artist's oil paint was discovered to paint flesh but I think it was developed to paint skies and clouds.

I'd like to be positive about gray—about all colors—but I'm not. When a gray sky gives way to blue it makes me happy. Of course, metaphorically gray is tiresome. Always in the way when snap judgments and quick prejudice should suffice.[3]

The Scale of Love

When we close our eyes to the landscape and think we have vanished, we find ourselves confronted with interior worlds. How do we measure the vastness of love, the scale of it?

I think about Pietro Rotari's eighteenth-century painting *Portrait of a Young Girl Hiding Her Eyes*. Note the title does not say weeping or blushing. I encountered this painting at the Palazzo Barberini in Rome in 2008. Before we were able take pictures freely in museums, I think we spent more time standing, studying, seeing. Even at the door on my way out, I hesitated and went back to look at it again. I was grieving the death of my father. This small painting captured that; it was more than grief expressed in soft gray. It portrayed not an image of sorrow, nor an image of shame, but a woman looking inward. It quickly became abstract on second seeing, a study of surface, of fabric, light—elements that might comfort.

Eyes hidden from the viewer, this image is full of mystery: what is she concealing behind that handkerchief—lavishing in her own interior world, perhaps with joy and not doom. I think about Wendy Beckett's description of Martin's art:

*Agnes Martin often speaks of joy; she sees it as the desired con-
dition of all life. Who would disagree with her?... No one who has
seriously spent time before an Agnes Martin [painting], letting
its peace communicate itself, receiving its inexplicable and inef-
fable happiness, has ever been disappointed. The work awes, not
just with its delicacy, but also with its vigor, and this power
and visual interest are something that has to be experienced.*[4]

But in that, is there a suffering *from* the yearning to obtain joy? A sorrow in the desire? An escape in the vastness and comfort in the control?

Fenton Johnson concludes in "Going It Alone" that indeed "A Solitary exists—in a continual opening to the possibility and grandeur of love."

I close with this list of Martin's titles:

Contentment
Far Away Love
Happiness
Innocent Happiness
Perfect Happiness
Innocent Love
Loving Love
LOVE

Originally printed in Agnes Martin: Independence of Mind *(Radius Books, 2022), 87-92.*

Epigraph: Undated lecture notes, facsimile insert between pages 16-17 of Arne Glimcher, *Agnes Martin: Paintings, Writings, Remembrances* (Phaidon, 2012), 13-14, 25. Reprinted in Nancy Princenthal, *Agnes Martin: Her Life and Art* (Thames & Hudson, 2015), 261.

1   Barbara Haskell, "Agnes Martin: The Awareness of Perfection," in *Agnes Martin* (Whitney Museum of American Art and Harry N. Abrams, 1992), 106.

Quoted from notes in the Arne Glimcher files, Pace Gallery, Boston.

2   Johannes Itten, *The Art of Color: The Subjective Experience and Objective Rationale of Color*, trans. Ernst van Haagen (Von Nostrand Reinhold, 1973), 46. Originally published in German, 1961.

3   Robert Gober, personal communication with author.

4   Wendy Beckett, *Sister Wendy's American Masterpieces* (DK, 1999), 77.

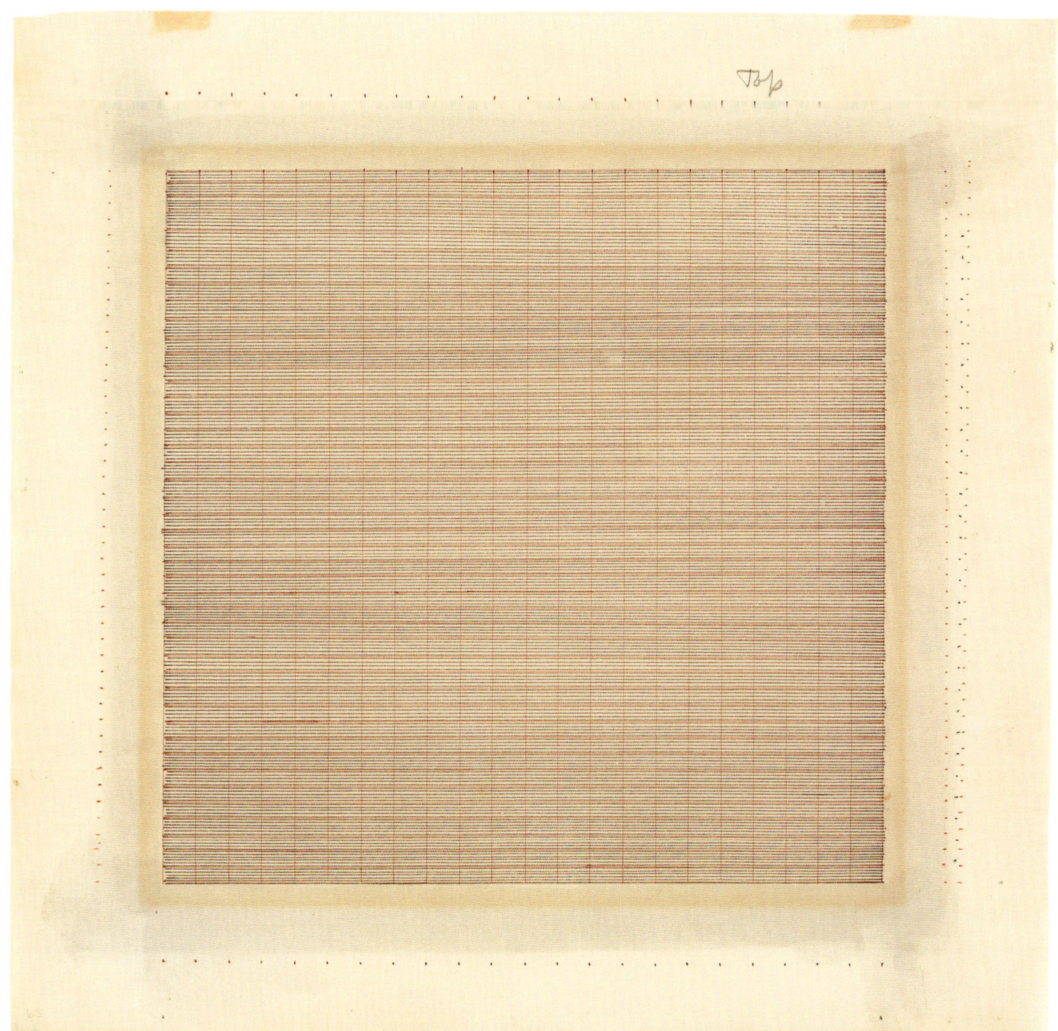

Agnes Martin, *Untitled*, 1963

Pen and ink, brush and ink, and wash on paper, 11¹³⁄₁₆ × 11¹⁵⁄₁₆ inches (30 × 30.3 cm)

Whitney Museum of American Art, New York; Gift of the Walter family in honor of May E. Walter

Fred Eversley, *Untitled (parabolic lens)*, **1970**
Cast polyester, 19½ × 19½ × 5⅝ inches (49.5 × 49.5 × 14.3 cm)
Private collection

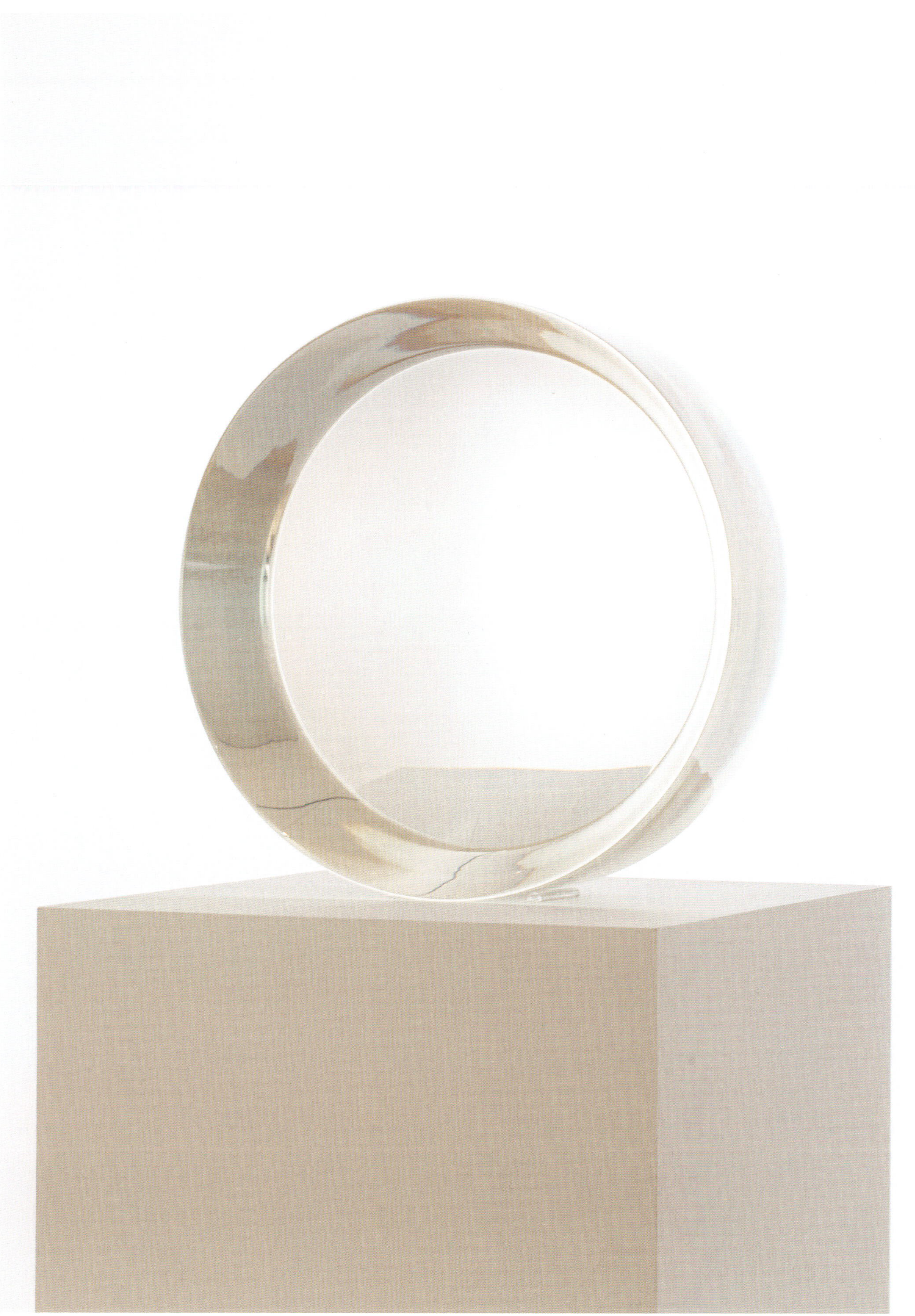

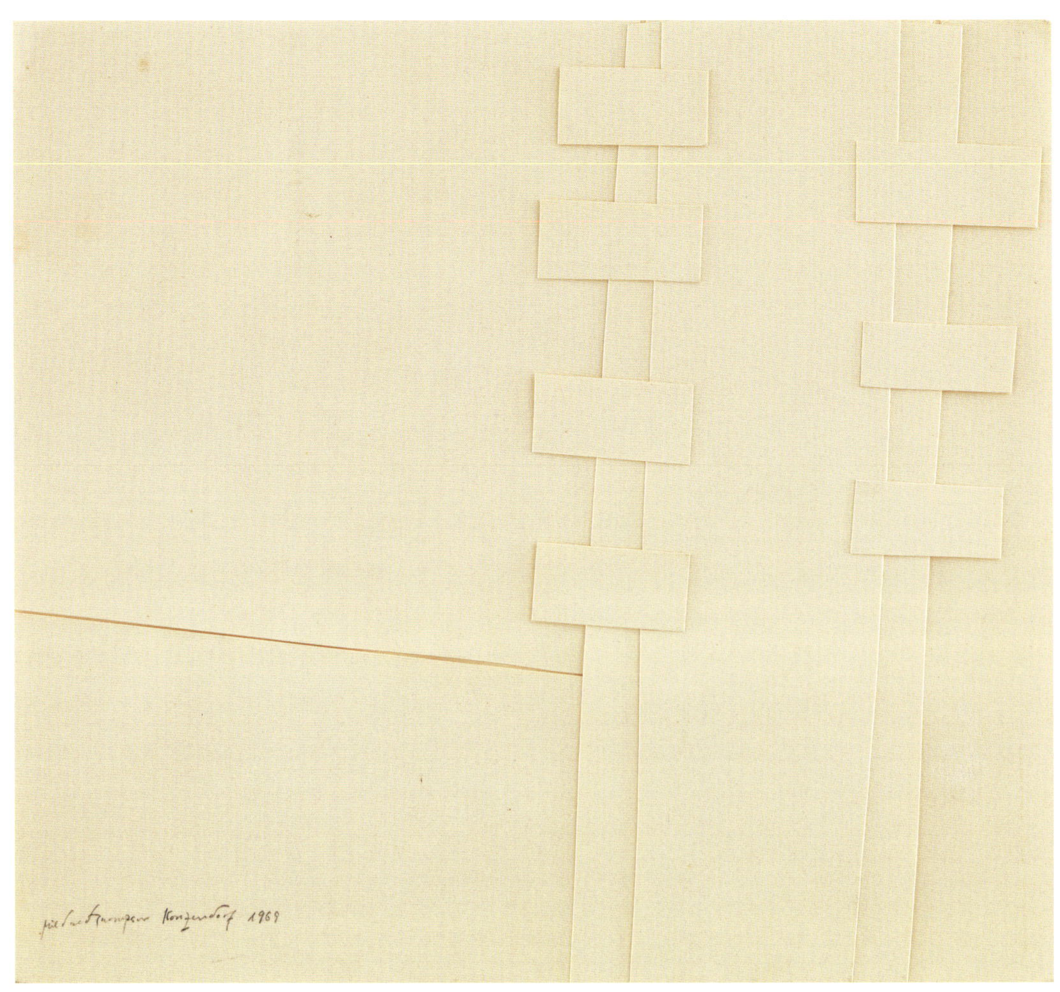

Mildred Thompson, *Untitled*, 1969
Paper collage, 8⅛ × 8⅝ inches (20.6 × 21.9 cm)
Private collection

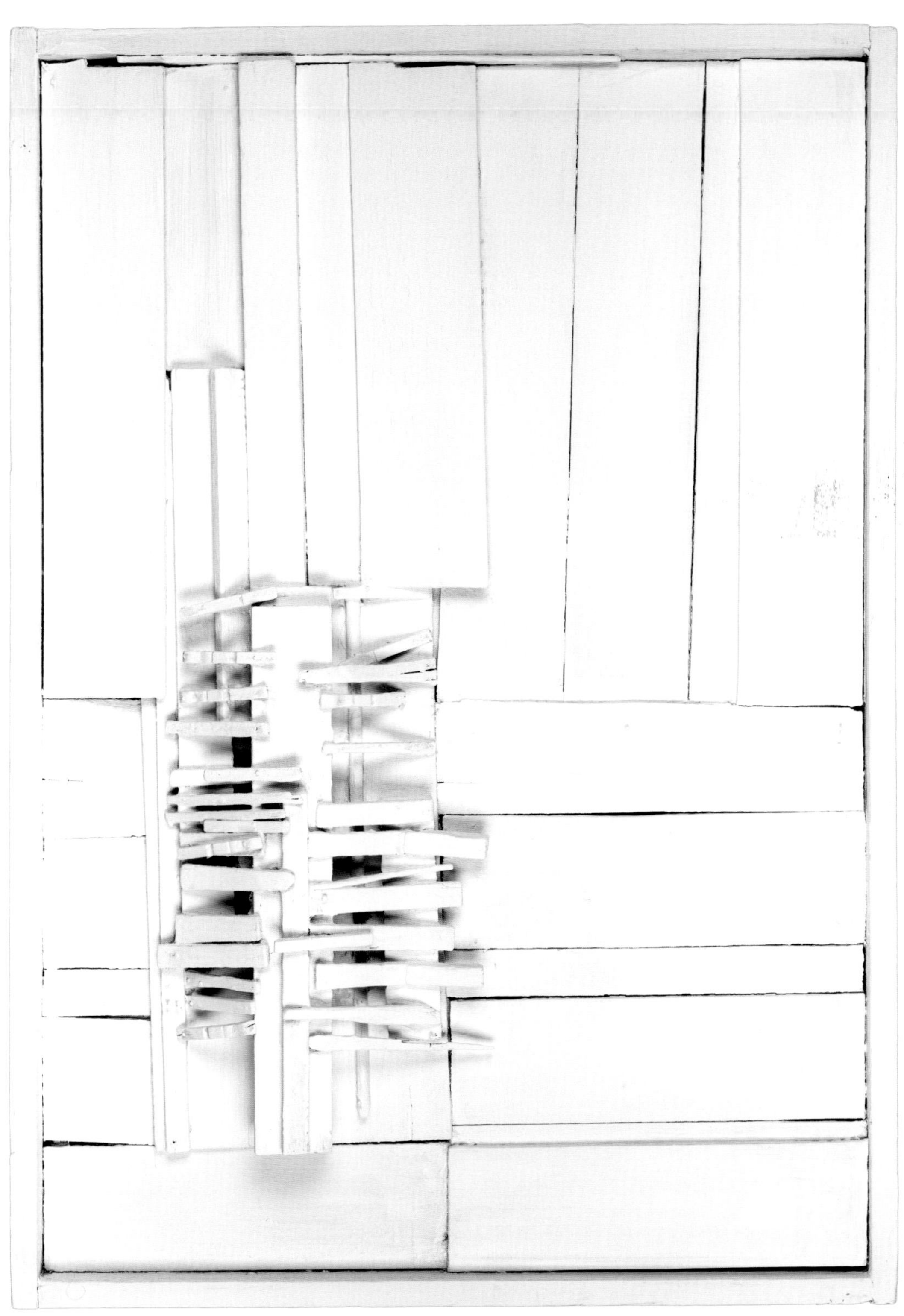

Mildred Thompson, *Wood Picture*, ca. 1966
Found wood and acrylic paint, 39⅜ × 27⅛ × 2⅜ inches (100 × 68.9 × 6 cm)
New Orleans Museum of Art, Museum Purchase, Leah Chase Fund

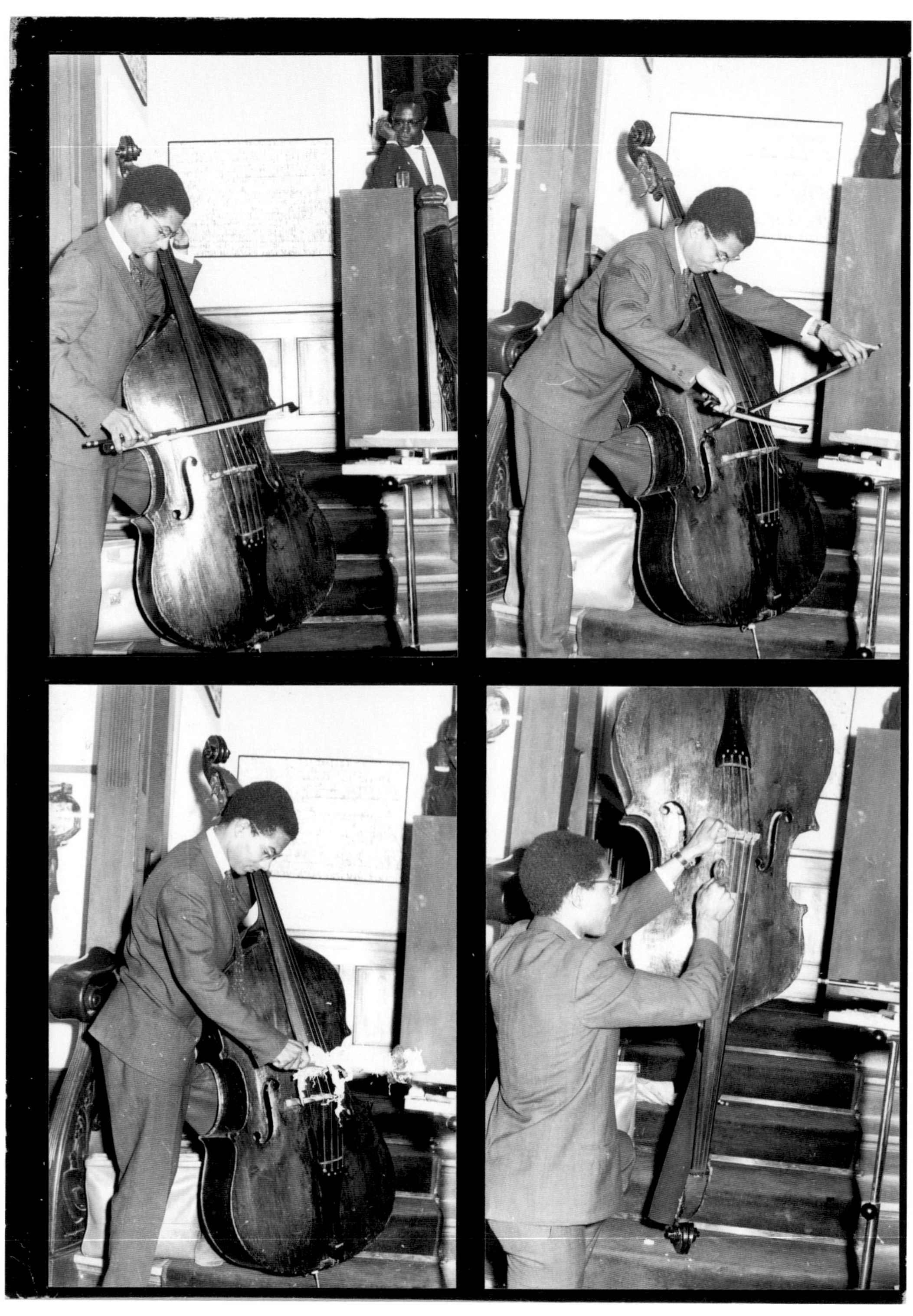

Benjamin Patterson, *Variations for Double-Bass* and *Duo for Voice and a String Instrument*, performed during *Kleines Sommerfest: Après John Cage*, Galerie Parnass Wuppertal, West Germany, June 9, 1962

Facsimile, printed 2025 from original gelatin silver prints on board, 10⅞ × 7¹¹⁄₁₆ inches (27.6 × 19.5 cm)
The Museum of Modern Art. The Gilbert and Lila Silverman Fluxus Collection Gift

VARIATIONS FOR DOUBLE-BASS

benjamin patterson

pitches, dynamics, durations and number of sounds to be
produced in any one variation in this composition are not
notated. (in the first performance by the composer a graphic
score derived from ink blots was used as a guide; however,
there are many other satisfacory solutions.)

I.

unfold world map on floor. circle with pen, pencil, etc. city
in which performance is being given. locate end pin of bass
in circle.

II.

using four different toy whistles, animal or bird imitators or
calls, etc. tune strings of bass as well as possible.

III.

produce a number of arco, quasi-webern sounds.

IV.

place a number of wooden and plastic spring-type clothespins
on strings several inches above bridge in such a manner that
they rattle and/or produce odd tones. arco; tremelo, trills
and/or long tones.

V.

weave strips of gold-face paper through strings in space
between bridge and fingerboard. fasten four colorful plastic
butterflies to strings over gold paper. performing normal,
"bartok" and/or "fingernail" pizzicati, catapult butterflies
from strings.

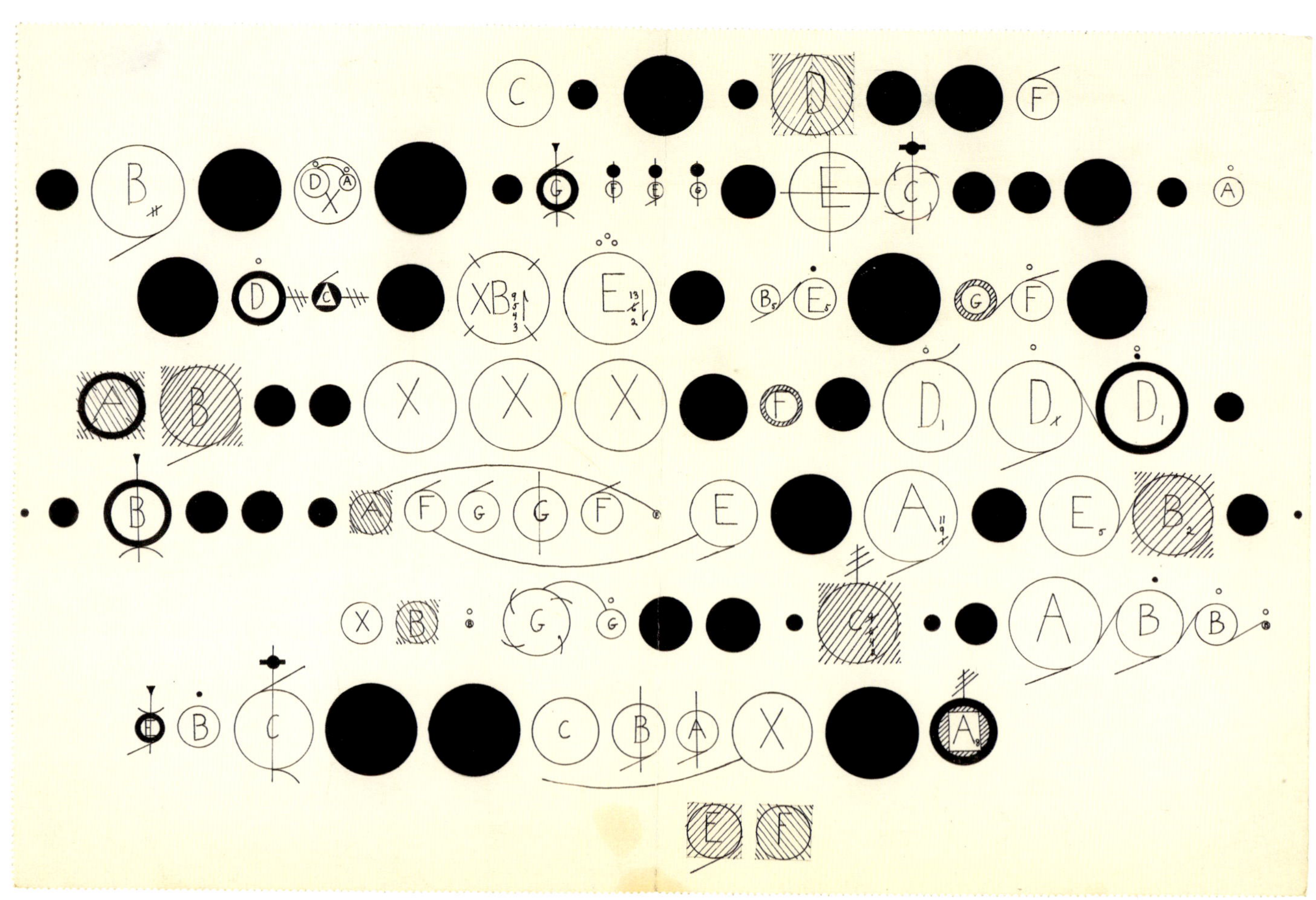

Benjamin Patterson, *String Music*, 1960

Facsimile, printed 2025 from an original black ink on folded paper, 10¾ × 16 inches (27.3 × 40.6 cm)
Getty Research Institute, Los Angeles

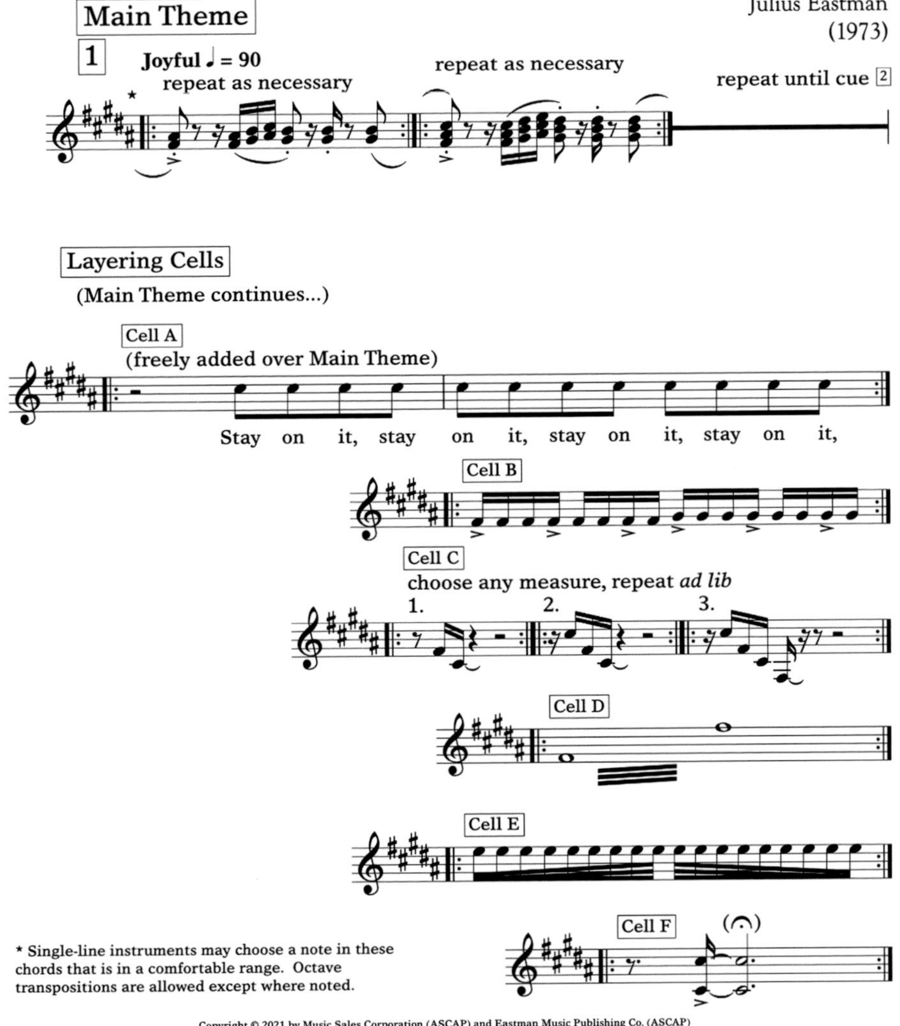

Julius Eastman, Score for *Stay On It*, 1973

12 × 18 inches (30.5 × 45.7 cm)

Distributed by G. Schirmer and Wise Music Group

Collection of Jennie C. Jones

Zarina, *Wall*, 1969
Relief print from collaged wood, printed in burnt umber on Indian handmade paper, 21⅞ × 28 inches (55.6 × 71.1 cm)
Whitney Museum of American Art, New York; Purchase, with funds from the Print Committee

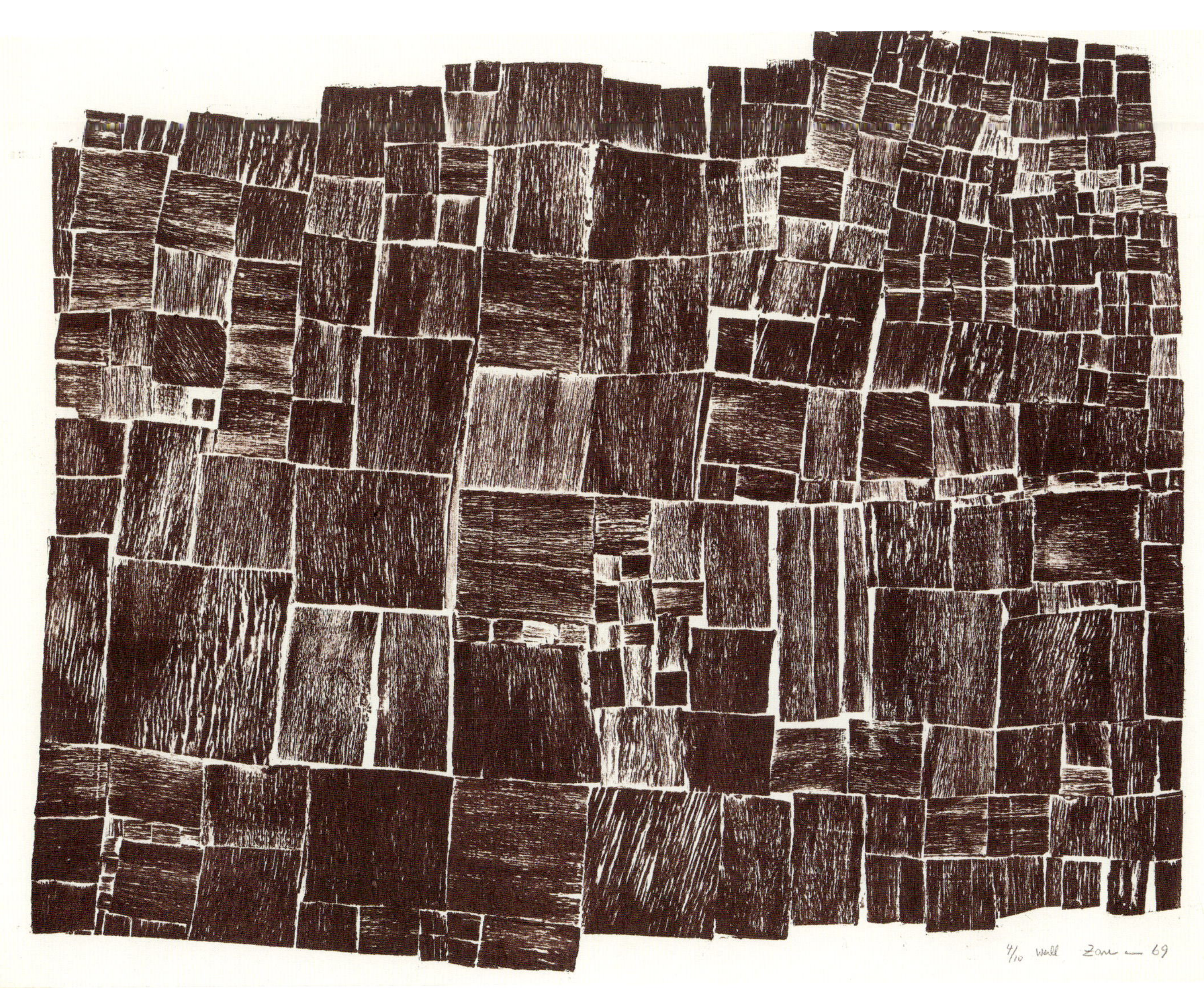

4/10   Wall   Zorn 69

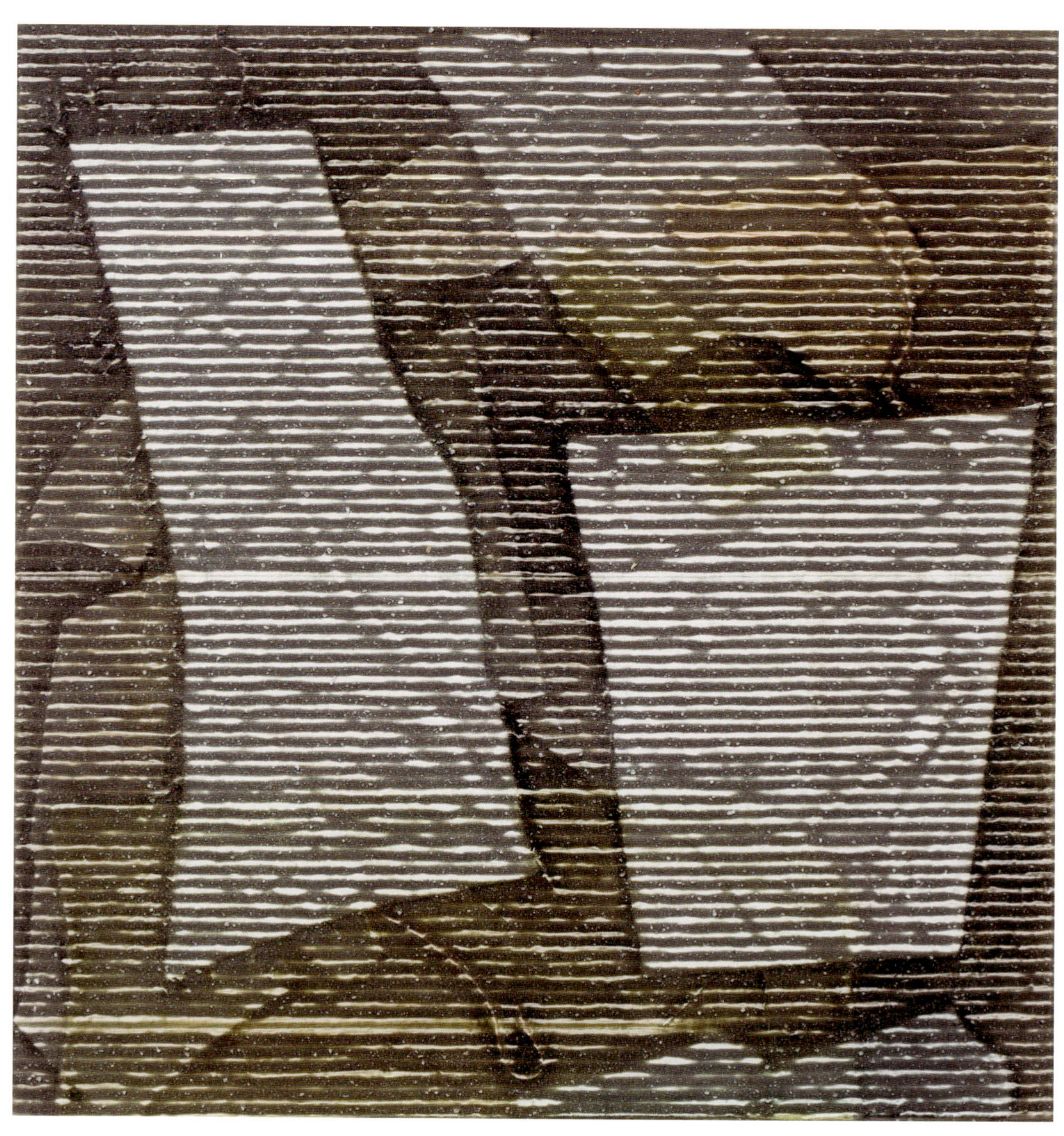

Jack Whitten, *Psee II*, 1978

Acrylic on canvas, 17 × 16 inches (43.2 × 40.6 cm)
Collection of Lizbeth and George Krupp

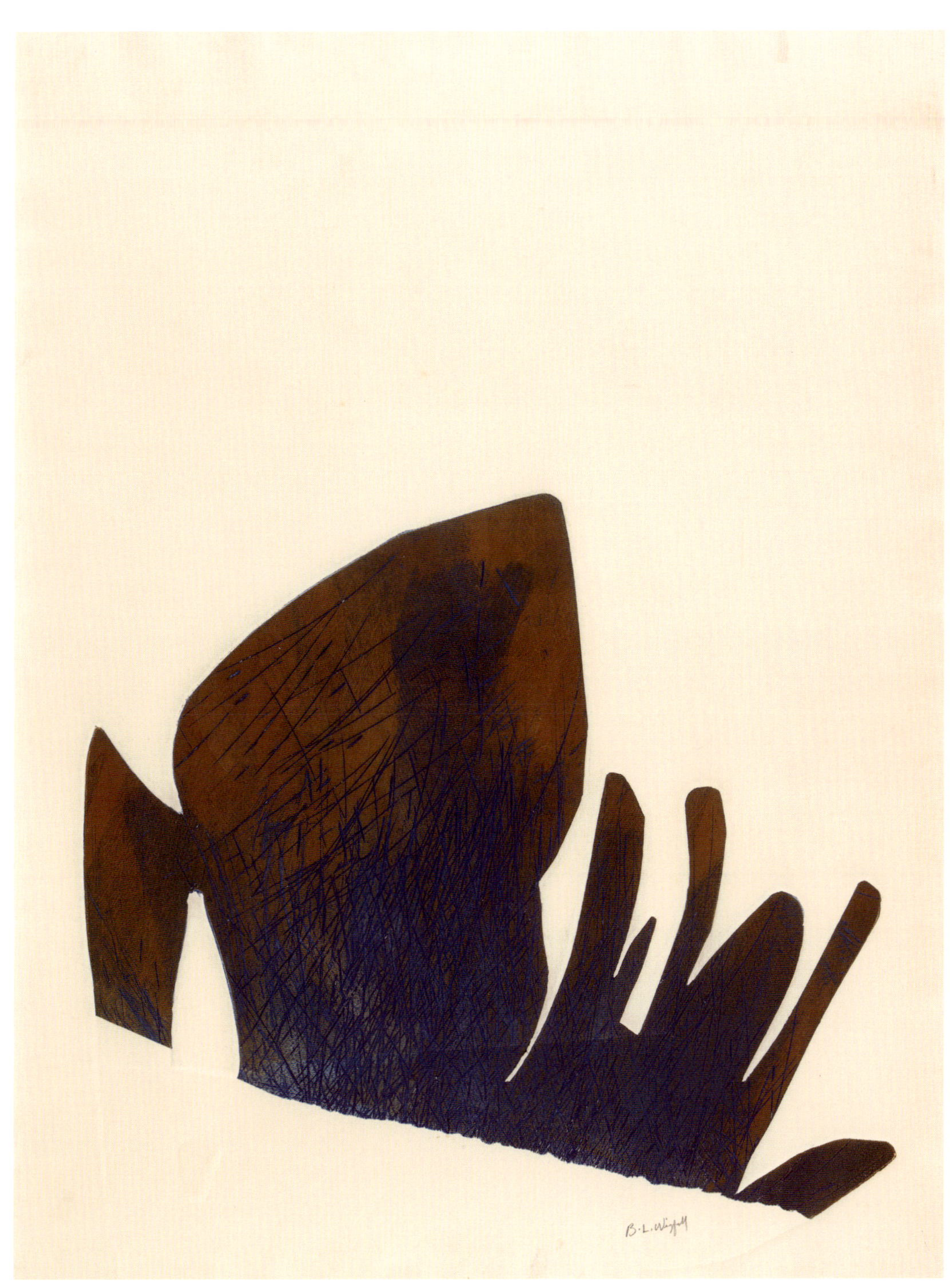

Benjamin Wigfall, *Nine Part Black Theme*, 1971

Etching on Arches wove paper, 30 × 22¼ inches (76.2 × 56.5 cm)
Virginia Museum of Fine Arts, Richmond. Arthur and Margaret Glasgow Endowment

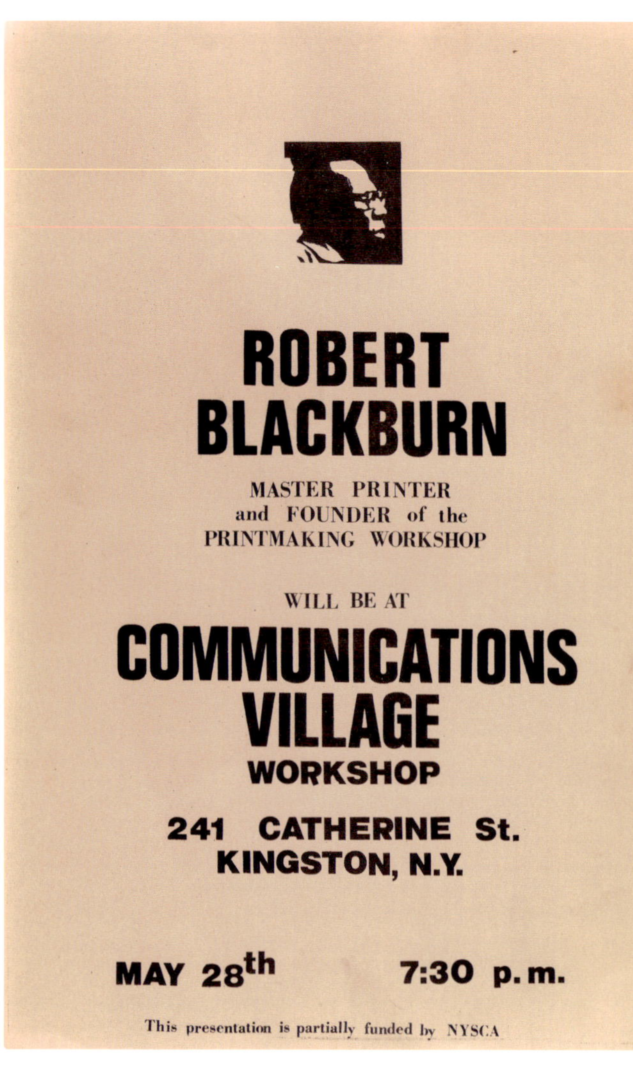

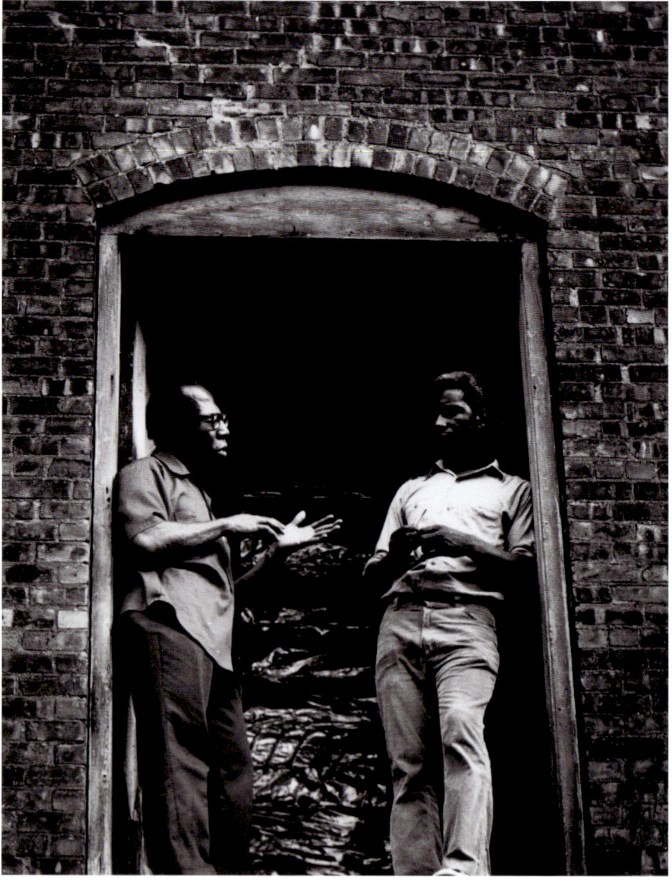

Communications Village Ltd., *Robert Blackburn, Master Printer and Founder of the Printmaking Workshop will be at Communications Village Workshop*, 1974–78

Poster, 17 × 11 inches (43.2 × 27.9 cm)
Virginia Museum of Fine Arts, Richmond, Margaret R. and Robert M. Freeman Library, VMFA Archives, Richmond, Virginia

Rose Tripoli, *Untitled (Robert Blackburn and Benjamin Wigfall in Doorway of CV [Communications Village])*, ca. 1974–76

Silver gelatin print on wove paper, $9\frac{15}{16} \times 7\frac{7}{8}$ inches (25.2 × 20 cm)
Virginia Museum of Fine Arts, Richmond, Arthur and Margaret Glasgow Endowment

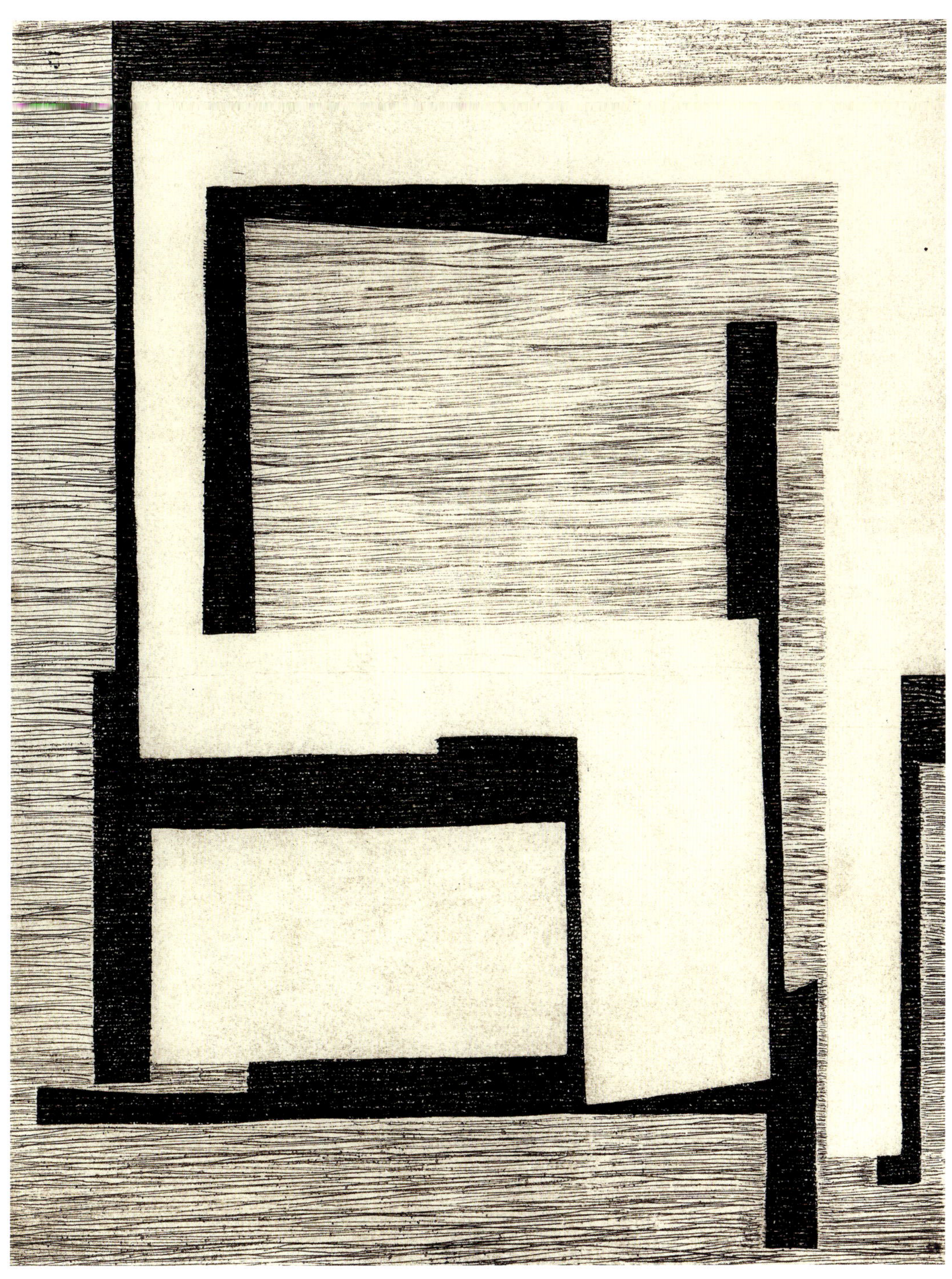

Mavis Pusey, *Quiet Movement*, 1965
Etching and aquatint on paper, 12 × 9 inches (30.5 × 22.9 cm)
Petrucci Family Foundation Collection of African American Art

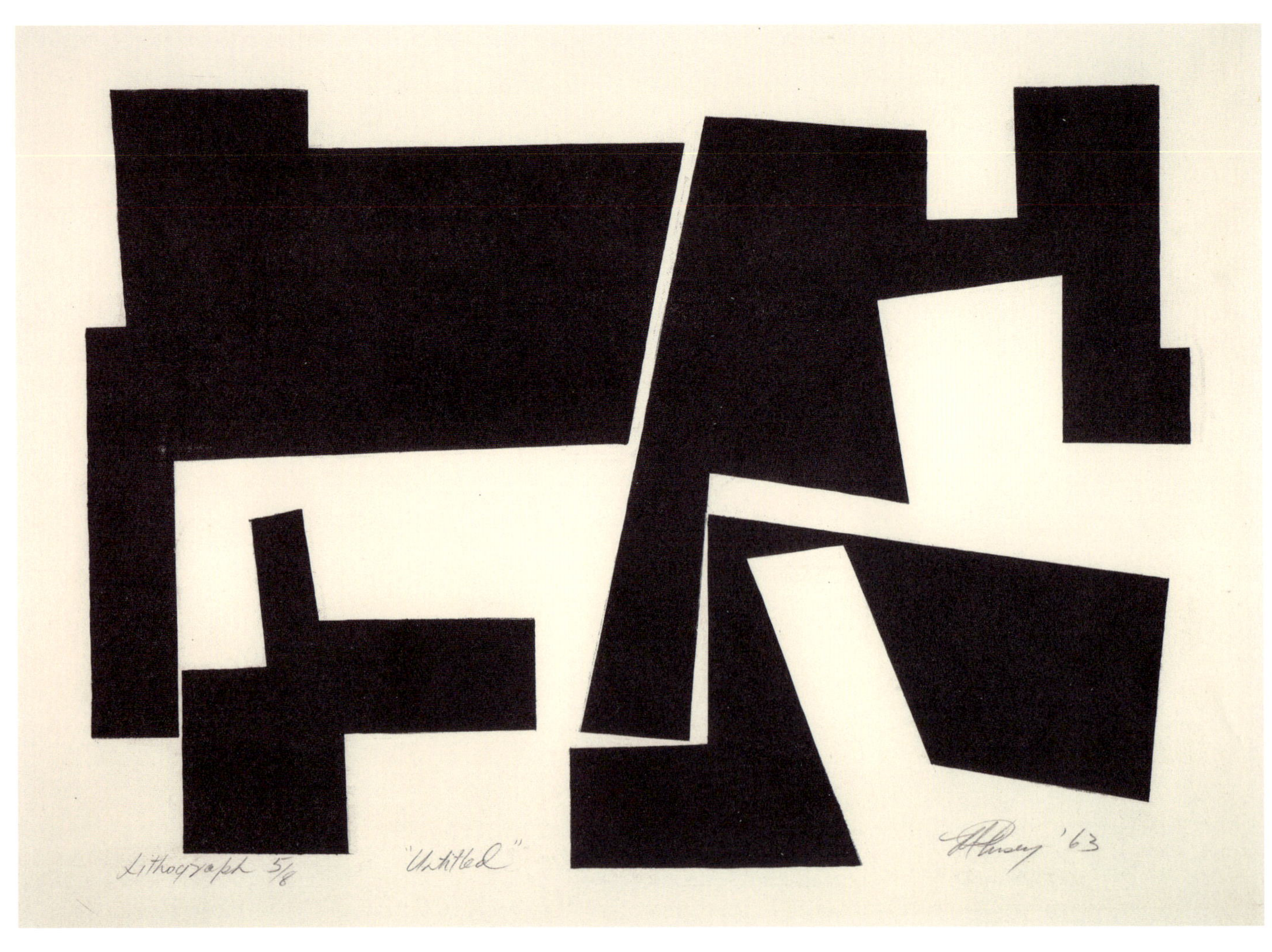

Mavis Pusey, *Untitled (Abstract)*, 1963

Lithograph on wove paper, 10⅝ × 14¹⁵⁄₁₆ inches (27 × 38 cm)

National Gallery of Art, Washington, Reba and Dave Williams Collection, Gift of Reba and Dave Williams

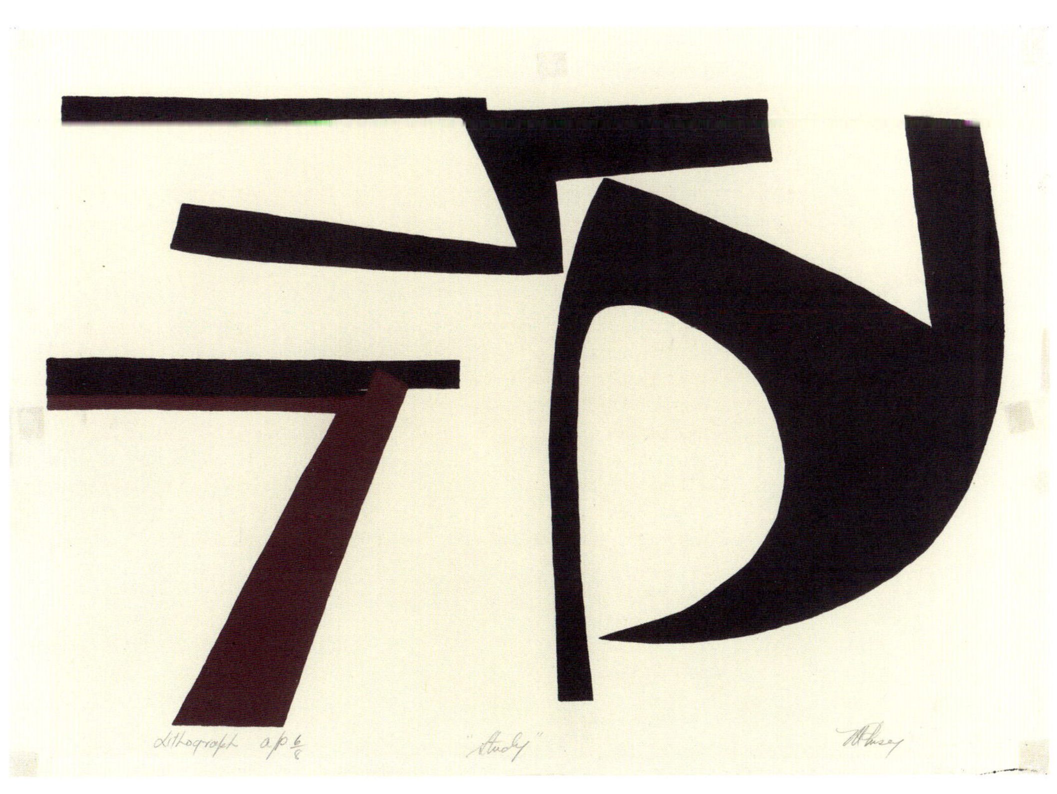

Mavis Pusey, *Study*, ca. 1970
Lithograph on wove paper, 15⅛ × 20¾ inches (38.4 × 52.7 cm)
Virginia Museum of Fine Arts, Richmond, Aldine S. Hartman Endowment Fund
and National Endowment for the Arts Fund for American Art

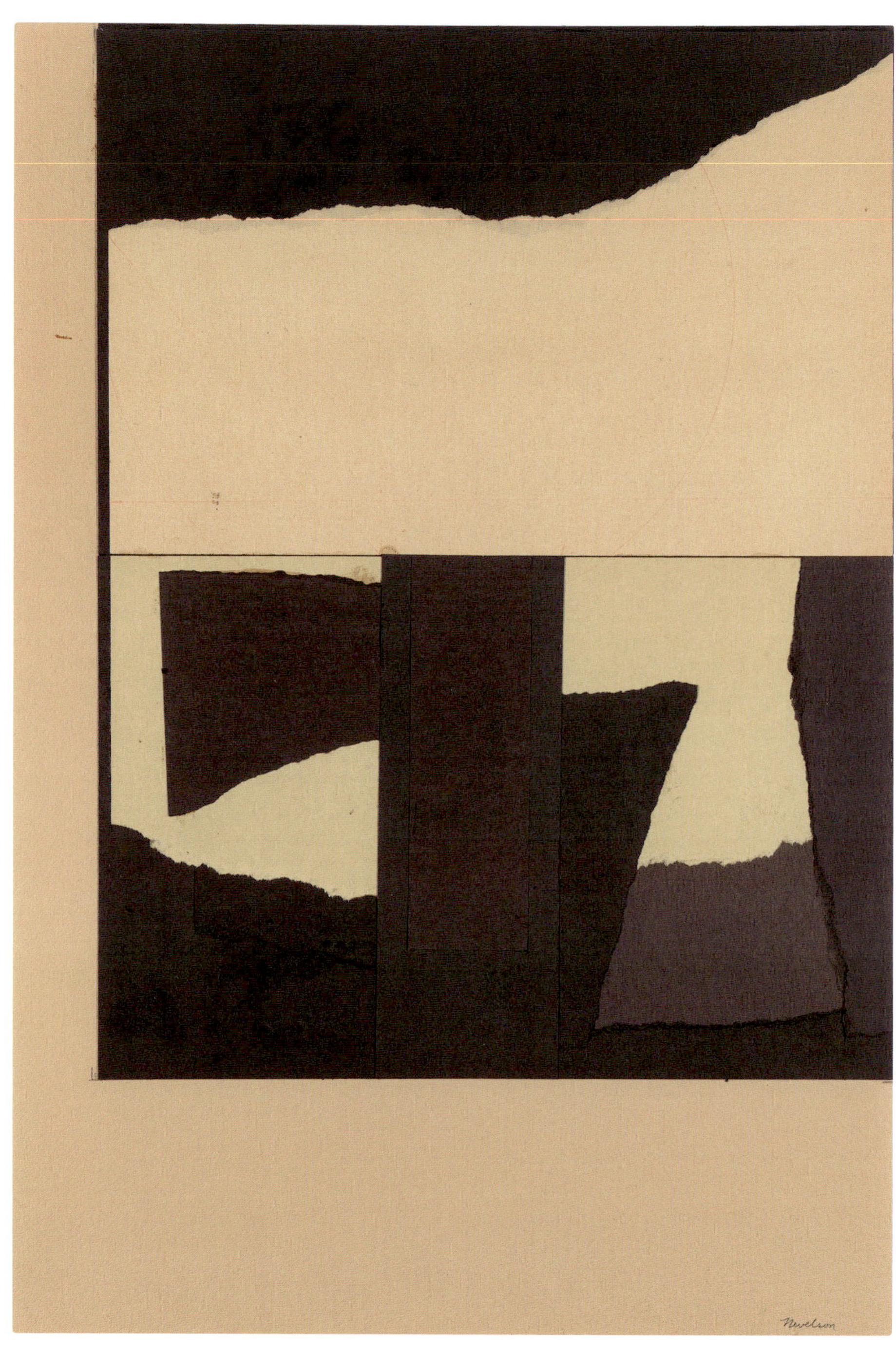

Louise Nevelson, *Untitled*, 1972

Paper collage and colored pencil on board, 29¹⁵⁄₁₆ × 20 inches (76 × 50.8 cm)
Whitney Museum of American Art, New York; Gift of Jean and Howard Lipman

JENNIE C. JONES

For most of Louise Nevelson's life, critics and admirers were virtually fixated on her use of the color black, and Nevelson did not circumvent addressing its importance. "I fell in love with black, it contained all color. It wasn't a negation of color. It was an acceptance. Because black encompasses all colors ... You can be quiet and it contains the whole thing."[1]

Early on, Nevelson imposed on herself parameters as a way to structure her works. The use of black and white was a form of restriction and discipline— or perhaps it was exactly the converse, a liberation—but, in any case, the lack of color became part of her signature style. "You see, [black] says more for me than anything else. In the academic world, they used to say black and white were no colors, but I'm twisting that to tell you that for me it is the total color. It means totality. It means: contains all."[2]

Interest in the meaning behind the use of this color has persisted. Pace Gallery's 2016 group exhibition *Blackness in Abstraction* attempted to unpack the complexities of blackness within various modes of visual art practice, though not so much as a conceptual or aesthetic strategy.[3] For me, the show, which included a small Louise Nevelson piece, landed flat: a curation via pigmentation without the depths the topic deserves. It ignored the complexities of the individuals in the exhibit and connected the works of art merely by the color of the pieces themselves.

Challenging on a different level was that the exhibition put forth a social political implication of the use of the color black by African Americans, who represented the majority of artists in the exhibition. Their blackness was reduced to a double entendre, as implied by the title, to simultaneously speak to the blackness of the maker and their cultural position. However, by juxtaposing these artworks and artists in relation to a different generation— those in "the canon" such as Nevelson, Rauschenberg, Reinhardt, LeWitt, and Sandback—what is implied here? Is one mode of black free within itself as an unencumbered aesthetic decision and the other somehow the embodiment of the diaspora? Is that curatorial position in itself a form of essentialism, making trite a much richer and more complex conversation?

In my own admiration of the color over the years, I too have projected all that I am—the depth of my identity— onto my black works. I know too well a form of double-consciousness in my own creative striving. When thinking about the works of Louise Nevelson, her bold, consistent, and skillful use of black offers something else, the notion of utilitarianism. Nevelson often referred to herself as "the original recycler," and she deconstructed and reused various parts of existing sculptures in new pieces.

This aspect of her methodology was different than, say, that of the intense editing and destruction of works by Agnes Martin. An example of the extremes of her process, this gave Martin total control, leaving a highly refined, edited oeuvre behind. Nevelson was far more fluid in her approach. In contrast to the structure of the pieces themselves, her decisions were dramatic. She turned things upside down, cut them in half, put parts in other parts. This aspect of her practice functioned almost like a heart transplant, offering new life to an old form. She recomposed "sentences" of forms into paragraphs that become installations. I believe her use of blackness as a conduit made this process possible. Blackness here is the sustainable thread, allowing all of her separate pieces over a lifetime to ease into one. Maybe this is what she meant when she said that blackness "is the totality." This form of assemblage, both in my own practice and pointed to in the title of this essay, is an idea of recomposition.

Score for Sustained Blackness is a series of a hundred works on paper that I began in 2014. Several of these collages would later intersect with Nevelson's work at the Rose Art Museum as a part of my Ruth Ann and Nathan Perlmutter residency in 2017, the fifty-year anniversary of her Rose exhibition. Expanding on the ideology and methodology of Louise Nevelson's artistic practice and spirit, excerpts from *Score for Sustained Blackness* were interpreted by Brandeis University student musicians. Creating a sonic presence for Nevelson's absent pieces (most were repurposed, no longer extant sculptures) the performance was a musical recomposition and instrumentation of Nevelson's "installation procedures." Her handwritten instructions provided an armature I could use to activate the works on paper as a true graphic score.

Perhaps this is what my work, and Nevelson's, proposes: that blackness knows how to endure, to adjust to move forward, to reposition and reassemble as a mode of survival. It is a metaphor that, acknowledging the necessity of blackness, offers a new entry into an overdue conversation.

Originally printed in Louise Nevelson: I Must Recompose the Environment *(Inventory Press, 2018),* 79-81.

1 Louise Nevelson, *Dawns + Dusks: Conversations with Diana MacKown* (Scribner, 1976), 126.

2 *Dawns + Dusks,* 125.

3 *Blackness in Abstraction,* Pace Gallery, New York. Curated by Adrianna Edwards, June 22–August 19, 2016. By contrast, the 2014 show *Black in the Abstract*—an ambitious, two-part exhibition at the Contemporary Art Museum in Houston, Texas, curated by Valerie Cassel Oliver—focused on African American artists working in geometric and nongeometric abstraction and color field painting. This cross-generational exhibition successfully tackled the huge subject of nonnarrative work by black artists.

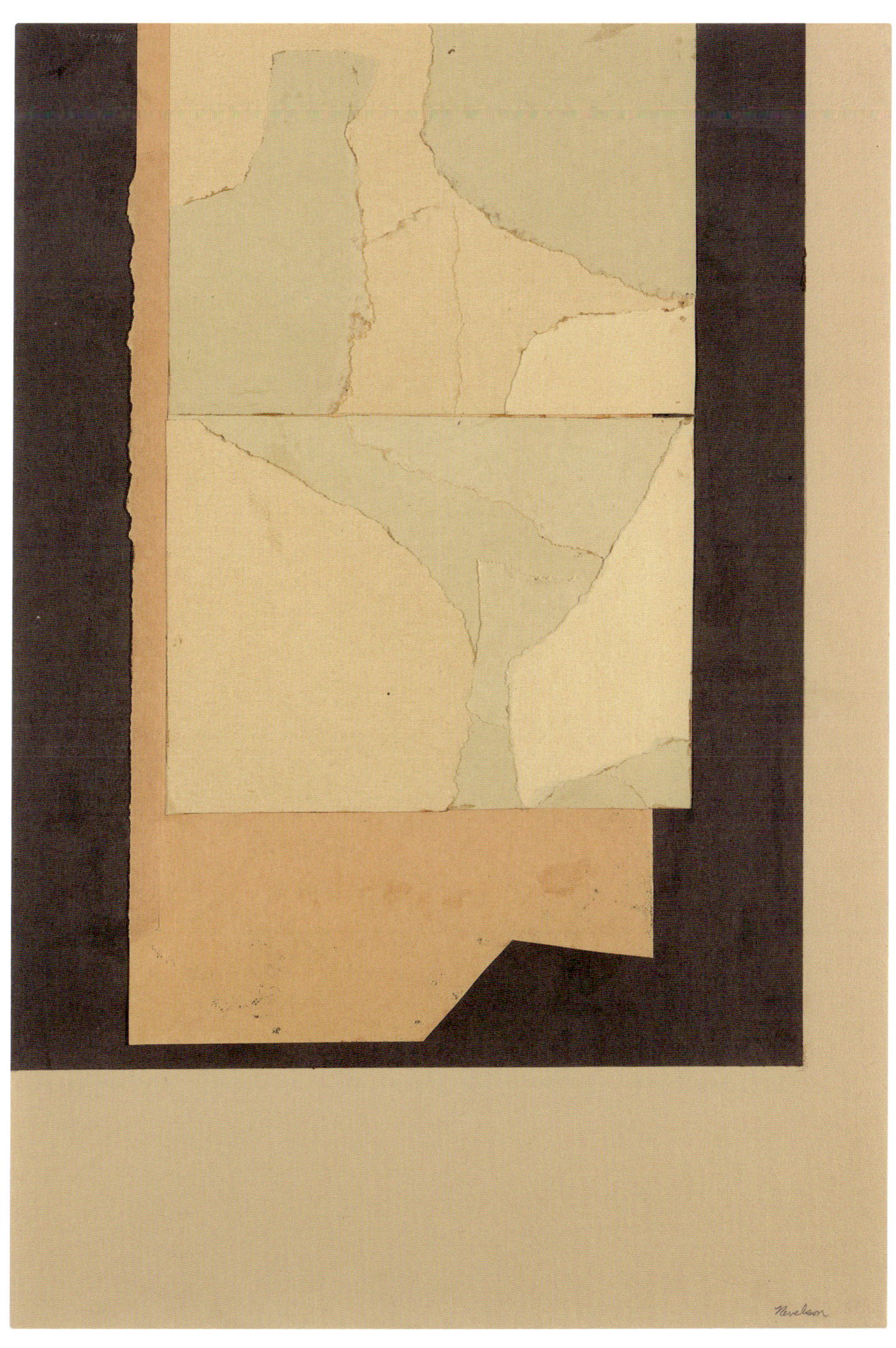

Louise Nevelson, *Untitled,* **1972**
Collage on paper, 29¹⁵⁄₁₆ × 20 inches (76 × 50.8 cm)
Whitney Museum of American Art, New York; Gift of Jean and Howard Lipman

Martin Puryear, *Métissage/Camouflage*, 2016
Woodcut on Torinko paper, 35⅝ × 47¾ inches (90.5 × 121.3 cm)
 Courtesy Universal Limited Art Editions

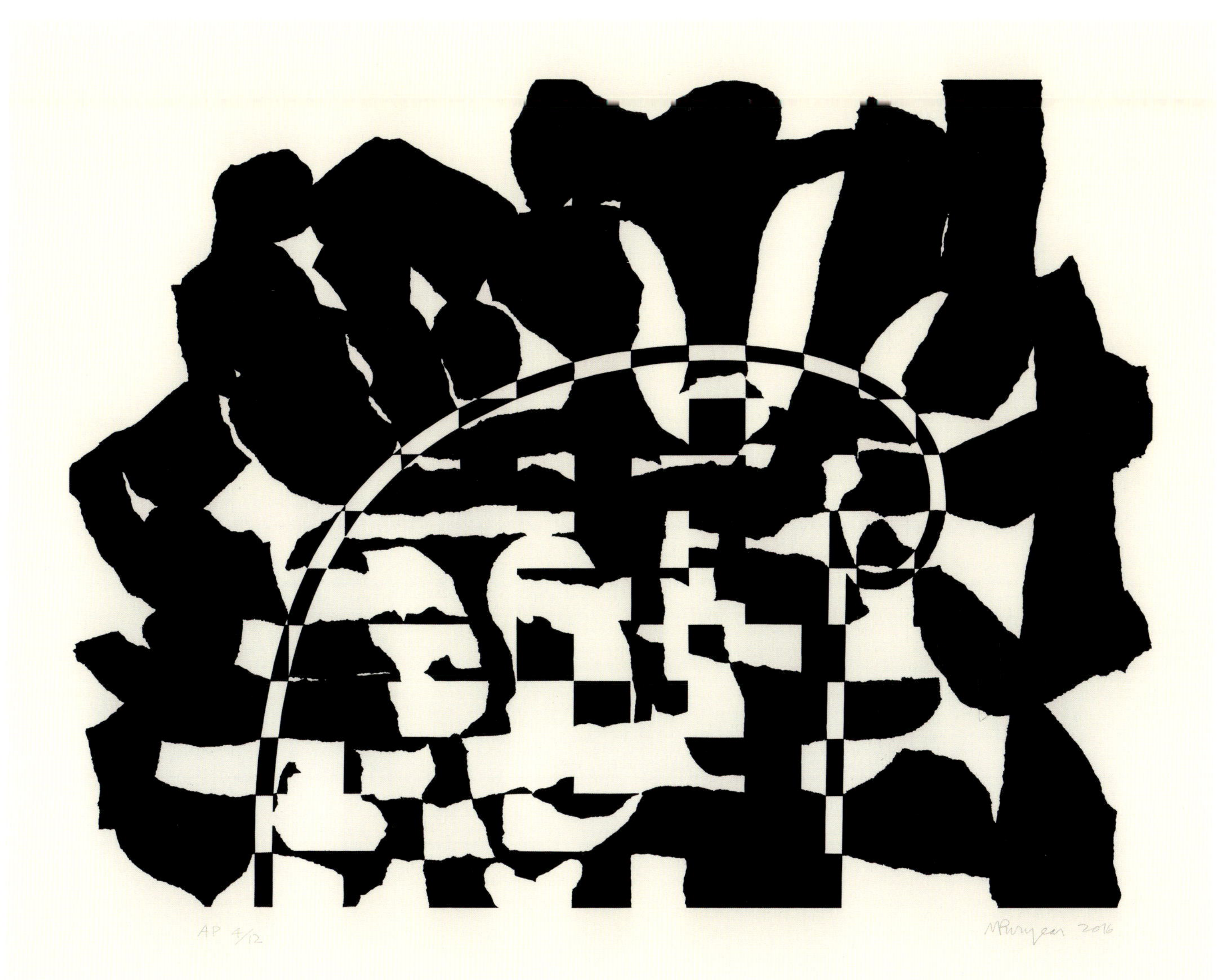

AP 4/12
NPuryear 2016

t de have s o n hat ce acean brai s are ver s m lar o u a b a n s exce t o t o o able d f e e ces, h c , t
m t i k n , act al make he cetacea b a n u e i r o u s. he f r t di ference a t d wt the s b let o
perce t o . H man be n s a e i e e ses; hey n o m he sel e abo t hei e v r n e t h o g s g t, o nd, t uch,
a te, a d me l. f ne sen e s o t an t e o ten beco e hei h e ed. I fac , b i d e r o s f e a pea t devel p an
en i e y e sen e. hes tate t cal th s e capac t "c m e sat r ," becau e t b i u l d e n t a e p o helso
s g t. Bu becau e i h i l s a o her awarenes o ten de el p — t e ab l t t act al perce ve t e resence f
o e h n w t o seen i . F r exam le, b i d e pe akn i a ield can o e o sen et a a ree s n r note ,
b ock n t e a .

I am o pe a ed t say he her hs e capac t t perce ve i w a we l ke t cal a " i t sen e," he her t s he
res l o l s e i g o ecl sel a d h sac ual y " ear g " he p e e ce o a objec a we a p oac i s g t e s, r het e
t e ind has he u devel ped r ubc n co s aci i y o e set e resence a objec t r u h he f rehead — a m s
radar- i e.

he u den able fac is, o e e , t i u ual y n a ped ca aci y does ex s i h man , a d hen e eed ar ses, t ca be
devel ped and ref ned. n ce acean , h wever, hs perce t a abi i y ex s s ead -made. W ae ' e e a e n he s des f
he r ead . T e e o e, hey a e w b i d p t i t er ield o v s o : o e d rec l a ead, here v s o i b ocked by he
h ge head; o e di ect y be nd t e hale, w e e i i n s n er ped b t e as f he b d . (T e hale s f lde day
t o advan a e f hs act and t o care t a p oac a a e r m di ect y as e n; hs a t e h ped o be n o i i n o
a e fect t i e i h h har o n be o e he w a e o iced t e r resence.)

ne as ect f he capac t t perce ve u see objec s s ex res ed i t e cetacea 's ab l t t "ech -l cate." B ief y u ,
t i mea s hat a cetacea l ca e a objec , o lea n h w a a ead f i a objec i , b e i t n a ou d n o he b i d
area (r an a ea, f r hat a ter), and men al mea u i t e i e hes u d a e t t a e f o h m, bo nce f t e
b ect, and retu n.

As e t o ed, t e e s a sec nd a ea i w ich he cetacea b a n and t e h man brai have s m lar t e yet di fer n
ca aci y. he sec nd d s inct o i m re d a a ic; becau e f t, a con i ced hat he cetacea ha a o e o hs ica ed
b an and a uch icher ap rec a in f i e v ro men t a wed . T e di t nct o i t i : T e ce acean brai has hat s
o n as a paral mbic l be, a d he h man brai d e n t. n he m s sm le te m , "para" mea s o e h n t a i
a o g ide o e h n ese; a d " i b c " ea s t s e a a e , di t nct, i h de i i e bo nda ies r bo der . I o he w rds,
he paral mbic l be i a e a a e obe, r a t f he b an — an add t o a par o t e brai w ich ce acean a o e a e.
Beca se we h man do o have s c a obe t s di f c l t e pan n u a ter s hat t s a d hat t does. n ode n
em , t e o a e fec m g t be t be ex lai ed as hat fac m u e .

T e ce acean' o e a l brai may be i e ed t t e co p e's e o y ba k. he w a e en e s n o as t a i n and s zes
t p i h all i sen e. T e da a a hered h o g t e e ses las i s a ty ho h he paral mbic l be, t e ear o t e
co p ter, u n n w a t e ndi id a sen e have perce ved n o ne m l i ace ed perce t o . T e hale s hen
co p e e y m e sed n ne s n le sen a i n hc we k o o l by e cei i g t c m o e t — separate, o e-at-a-t me
sen a i n . T e hale n tan l k o s hat hc a u a has o ar i e at ho g id cie ea o i g.

ne o t e hn s hat amazes e pe p n hei i t oduct o t he cetacea fam l i t e act hat hese mam a s a e
o nds and, t r ug t e e o nds, hey ca c m u ica e. n he case o t e male w a e — t e d l hn a d o p i e
— t e e o nds are a e ies f hs les and c icks. u a s ca hea s m e o t e e do p i s u d , b t he a i a s are
capab e o mak n t e e o nds at uch a h g f e uency hat hey are o t f u ra ge o hea i g. u a s ca hea u t
1 o e e 2 k l her z; do p i sca a e o nds, audible t eac o her, p a d t 1 0 io e t .

T e a ger he w a e, he o e o hs ica ed t e o nds hey a e ap ear o be. At ab u he s ze o t e io w a e
(o e han 5 eet) ce acean so c ick n a d s at a i g h oate , g t ier o nds. Al o, hales a e a dee e v ice
an e han u a s, o hei v ice can ravel a t e . T e u pback f a ai's i ter ae s n a t c lar a e ich
" o ces," n hc t e u ter ha have bee cal ed "s n s." ne m g t co s der se o t a w rd a i s a ce of an-
ho o o p i i g, bu D . R ger a ne, a e per o w ae o nds, ex lan t a t e od " o g " s sed beca se t e
u pback a e man var ed s unds hc a e t e ed i c m lete seq e ces. he seq e ces are repea ed o nd f r
o nd, a an and a a n. As o i h n l , s me o t e e uence can las f r wen y i u e. Pay e i d , a have o her
e earcher , t a t e m bac s n s chan e r m ear o ear n he same geo rap ica a ea a d d f e f o o e at f
he w rd o an t e . I w ud eem, n u a ter s, a t o g t e u pback have d f e e t a g a e i t e di feren
par s o t e ea w rd.

o e ce o o i t bel e e hat di feren s ecies f ha e can and d c m u ica e i h each t e , act al "tal " wt
eac o her. Yet each pece o w ae a is w d s i c s u d. he " v ice" f he h m back, s, bel e e, he m s
d s i c a d hem s d s i c ie. t ran e s fo t e e y i h, al o tas uea , t t e e y o , a bas po u d w ich
em g t ex ect a w a e o a e. hes n s f he h m bac s are del vered at t e e d u s eed . T o sands f y lab e
a d " od " a e t e ed i a ec nd.

From *Brother Whale* by Roy Nickerson

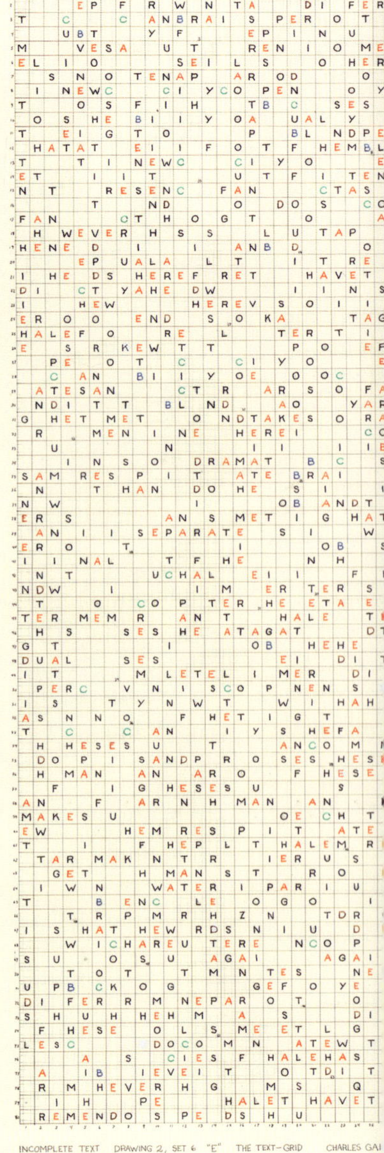

Charles Gaines, *Incomplete Text #6 "E,"* 1978–79

Photostat (a); pen and colored inks, correction fluid, and graphite pencil on paper (b); pen and colored inks
and graphite pencil on paper (c), 3 sheets, 27⅝ × 59¾ inches (70.2 × 151.8 cm)

Whitney Museum of American Art, New York; Gift of Meredith Palmer in honor of Adam D. Weinberg

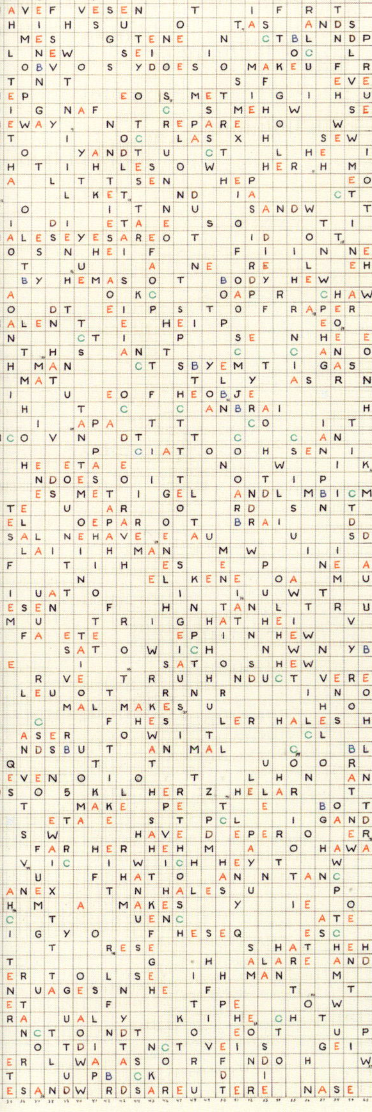

dies have hat ace an bra are la man bra able
.act make he ace an bra he has do the let
.man be have hey he el abo he men
.as and me an her ten be me he ten fa nap pea eve an
.new I he ate new cap pen sat be does make he
.be her aware ten el he act the
.met see exam a el can me hat a hem
.he way
.   I am par say he her new cap hat a sew he her he
.ten el and ear he fan as we he her
.in has he eve do fa hep fan he head
.radar
.   he den able fa is, ever tap pa does man sand hen an be
.eve and ace an ever la ad-made. hales eyes are he id
.he ad here hey have he el he ad here by he
.head; be he hale here by he ma he body he hale day
.ad van tag act and care a hale as way hey be
.a be hale iced he
.   as he cap see he ace an cat
.me an hat a ace an ate an far he ad man bye a he
.area an are hat mat and men me as he met he takes ravel he
.and
.   As men here a are he ace an bra and man bra have la yet
.pa he in drama be I am con hat he ace an a ate
.bra and a her at men an we do he he ace an bra has hat
.as a para be and he man bra does he "para" me an met hat
.id met gel and an separate he
.para be a separate be par he bra an add par he bra ace an have
.Be we man do have a be la man hat hat does. ode
.he tale be be la as hat a
.   he ace an era bra may be me an he hale a at and
.all he tag at here he as tan he para be he ear he
.hat he id have ace hale hen
.let el me sat we by – separate at-a me
.sat he hale tan hat a man has at duct as
.   he hat amazes he duct ace on fa he act hat he mam ma makes
.and he hey an ate he case ma hales do sand
.he are a and man an he me he do he an ma are
.cap ma he at a hat hey are an he man an he
.15 even 20 her do an makes audible her wards 150 her
.   he la he he ate he hey make ear be. At he hep hale
.an 15 ace an and tar ma oat hales have a ice
.an get an man he ice can ravel far her he back water par la have
.hey have bee id hat an tan an
.Dr. Pay anex hales la hat he be he
.back makes man are let he are pea
.and As me can la we Pay as have he
.archer hat he on ear ear he same rap are and par
.he an her man he back have an ages he
.par he
.   me be eve hat can and do ate each her act
.her yet each hale has ice back I be eve he
.and he ran ever a ever a as do
.a hale have he he are el red at men do sands lab
.and are a

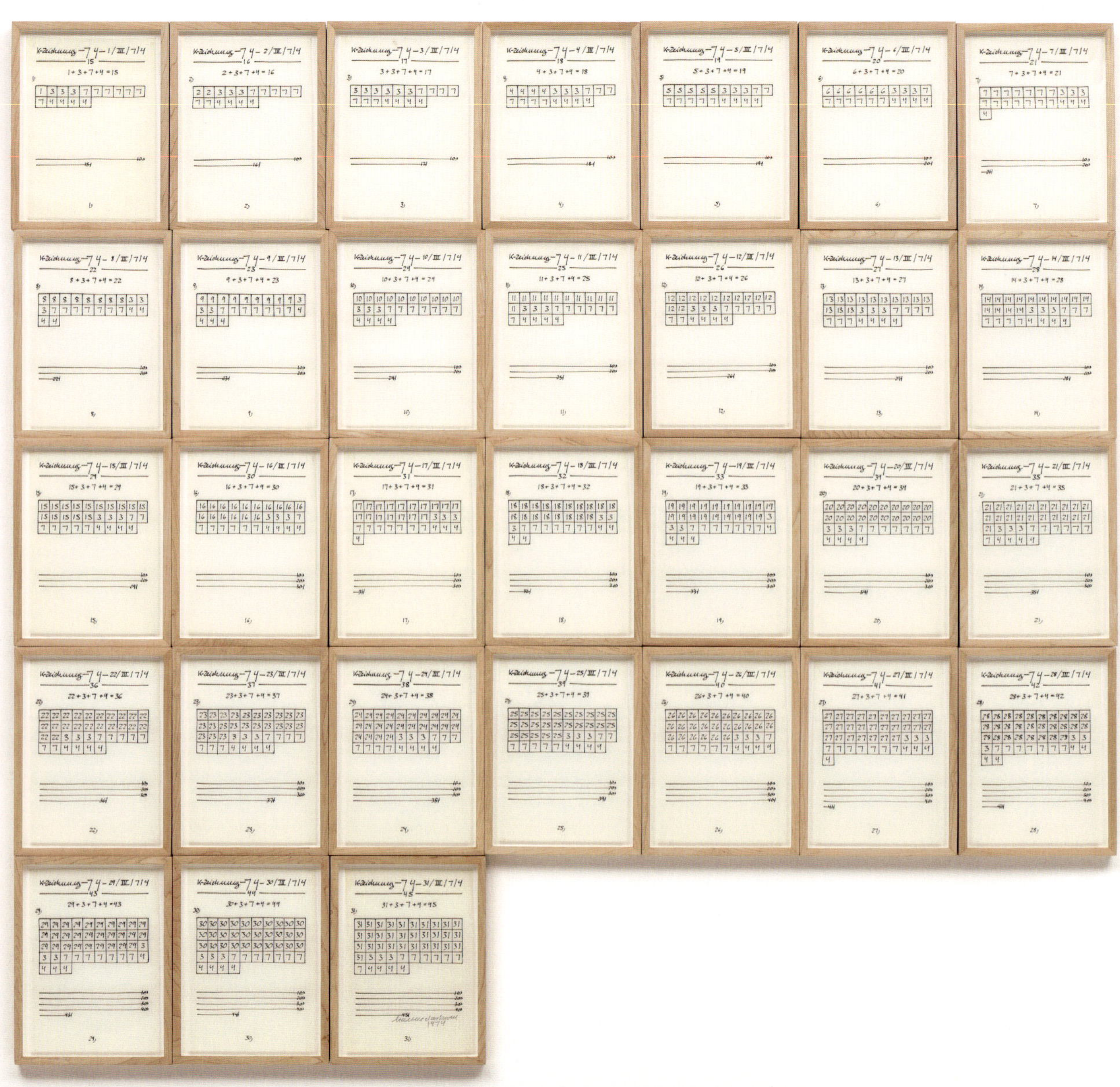

Hanne Darboven, *Month III (March)*, 1974
Ink on 31 pieces of transparentized paper, 66½ × 70 × 1½ inches (168.9 × 177.8 × 3.8 cm) installed
The Museum of Modern Art, New York. The Judith Rothschild Foundation Contemporary Drawings
Collection Gift, 2005

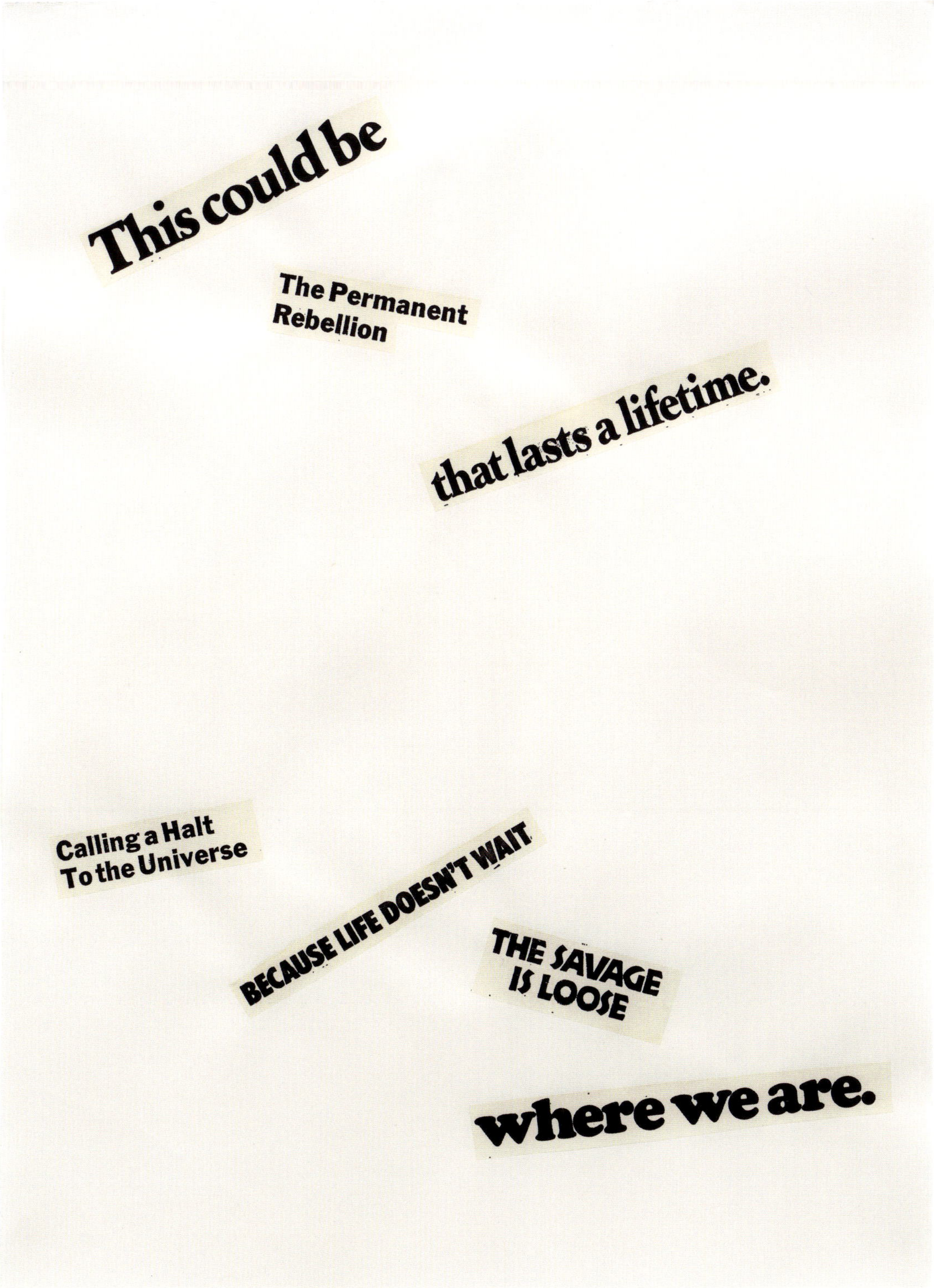

Lorraine O'Grady, *Cutting Out CONYT 26*, 1977/2017
Letterpress printing on Japanese paper, cutout, collage on laid paper, 41¾ × 29¾ inches (106 × 75.6 cm)
Courtesy Alexander Gray Associates, New York

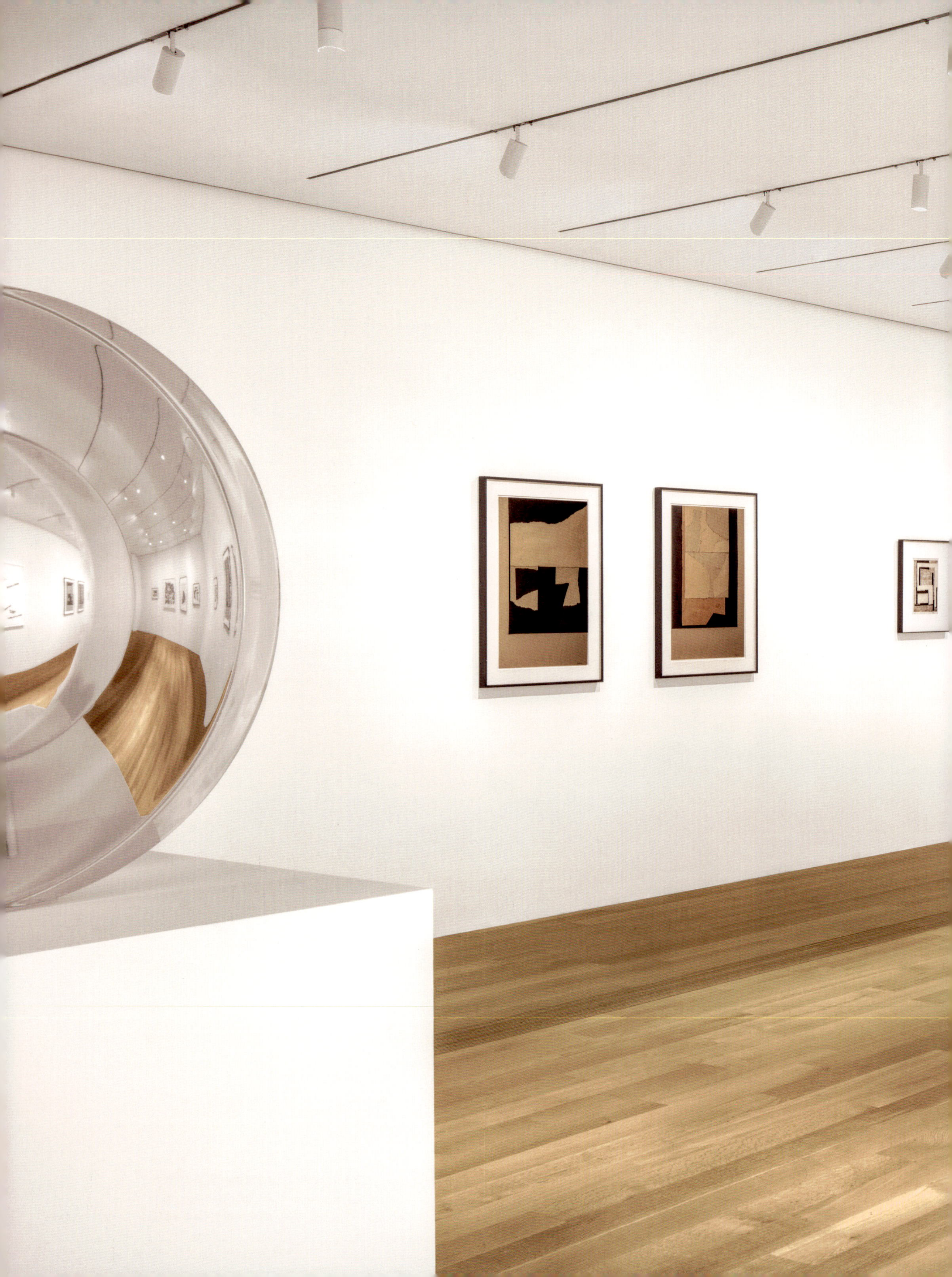

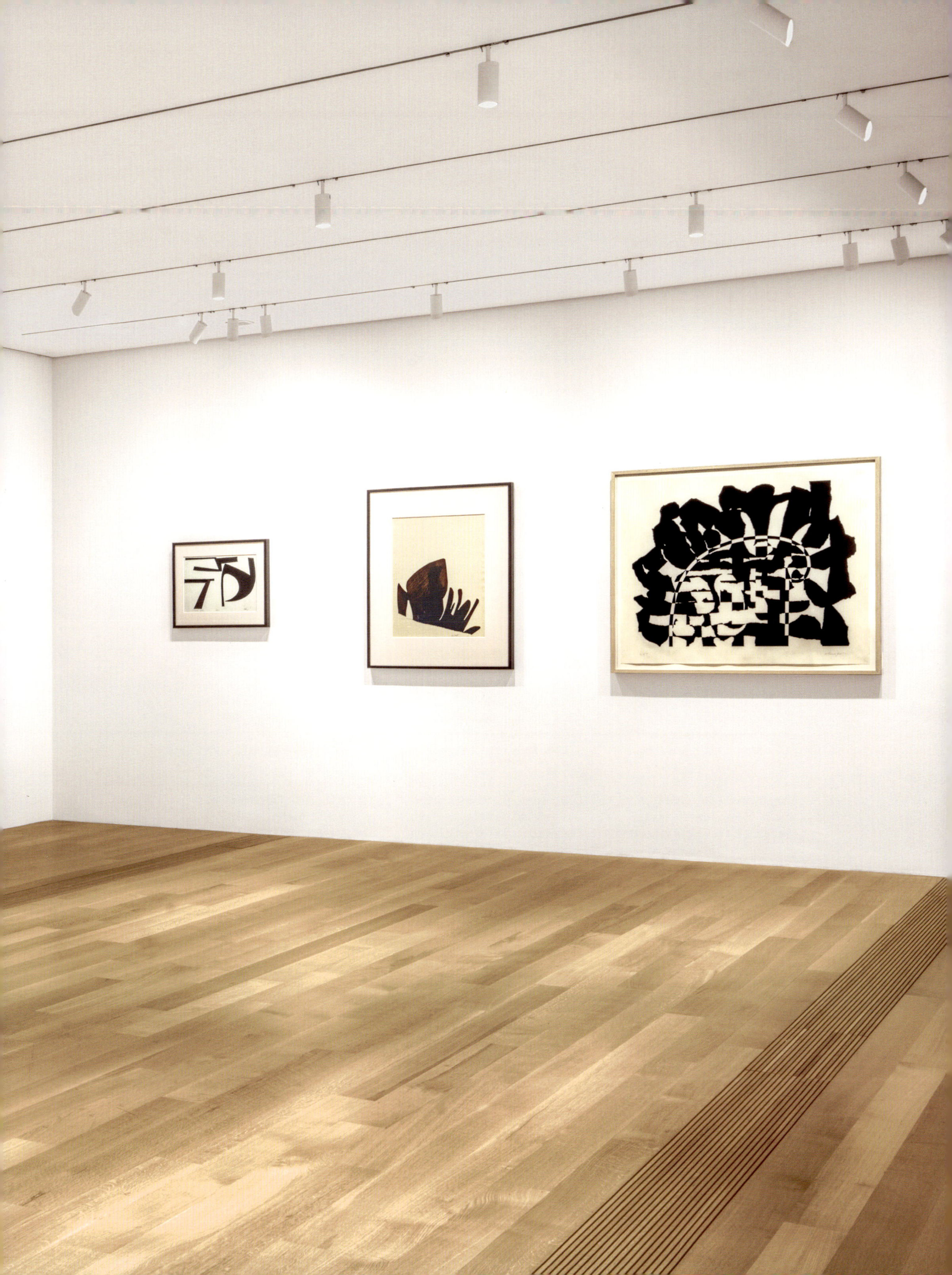

Jennie C. Jones: A Line When Broken Begins Again

**All works are by Jennie C. Jones, and courtesy Alexander Gray Associates, New York, unless otherwise noted.*

RPM (revolutions per minute),
2018
Digital sound piece
Running time 3:34 min.

Triple Bold Bar, End Measure,
2022
Acrylic, acoustic panel, and architectural felt on canvas in 2 parts
48 × 48 × 3½ inches (121.9 × 121.9 × 8.9 cm) each

Soft Sharps, Line Break, 2023
Acrylic, acoustic panel, and architectural felt on canvas
48 × 36⅛ × 3⅛ inches (121.9 × 91.8 × 7.9 cm)
The JLS Collection

A Line When Broken, 2025
Acrylic, acoustic panel, and architectural felt on canvas
48 × 36¼ × 3⅝ inches (121.9 × 92.1 × 9.2 cm)

Bass Notes with Leaning Hum,
2025
Acrylic on canvas, architectural felt, and acoustic panels
Part 1: 36 × 12 × 1½ inches (91.4 × 30.5 × 3.8 cm)
Part 2: 2½ × 11⅞ × 11⅞ inches (6.4 × 30.2 × 30.2 cm)
Part 3: 2⅛ × 24 × 24 inches (5.4 × 61 × 61 cm)
Part 4: 2⅛ × 24 × 24 inches (5.4 × 61 × 61 cm)

Complex Octaves Diptych #1,
2025
Acrylic on paper in 2 parts
25¾ × 19¾ inches (65.4 × 50.2 cm) each

Complex Octaves Diptych #2,
2025
Acrylic on paper in 2 parts
25¾ × 19¾ inches (65.4 × 50.2 cm) each

Deep Red, Black, 2025
Acrylic, acoustic panel, and architectural felt on board
30 × 30⅜ × 2½ inches (76.2 × 77.2 × 6.4 cm)

Floor Notation (red), 2025
Architectural felt
⅜ × 270 × 96 inches (0.9 × 685.8 × 243.8 cm)

Hushed with Black Red Edge,
2025
Acrylic, acoustic panel, and architectural felt on canvas
48 × 36⅜ × 2¾ inches (121.9 × 92.4 × 7 cm)

Interlude, 2025
Digital sound piece
Running time 1:15 min.

Long Low Rest with Hum, 2025
Acrylic, acoustic panel, and architectural felt on canvas
49⅝ × 48 × 3½ inches (126 × 121.9 × 8.9 cm)

Measured Earth Tone, 2025
Acrylic, acoustic panel, and architectural felt on canvas
48 × 48⅛ × 3¾ inches (121.9 × 122.2 × 9.5 cm)

Phrasing to the Floor, Softly, as in an Evening Sunset (for Nina),
2025
Acrylic and architectural felt on canvas and brass in 4 parts
Part 1: 48½ × 48 × 2½ inches (123.2 × 121.9 × 6.4 cm)
Part 2: 48 × 48 × 2 inches (121.9 × 121.9 × 5.1 cm)
2 brass blocks: 2 × 2 inches (5.1 × 5.1 cm) each

Point of Perspective, 2025
Wood, MDF, acrylic paint, and architectural felt
142 × 36 × 148 inches (360.7 × 91.4 × 375.9 cm)

Soft Tone with Red Break, 2025
Acrylic, acoustic panel, and architectural felt on canvas
48 × 48⅛ × 3⅝ inches (121.9 × 122.2 × 9.2 cm)

Two Hushed Movements (Diptych), 2025
Acrylic, acoustic panel, and architectural felt on canvas
12 × 12½ × 2½ inches (30.5 × 31.8 × 6.4 cm) each

Other Octaves: Curated by Jennie C. Jones

Communications Village Ltd. (active 1970s)
Robert Blackburn, Master Printer and Founder of the Printmaking Workshop will be at Communications Village Workshop, 1974–78
Poster
17 × 11 inches (43.2 × 27.9 cm)
Virginia Museum of Fine Arts, Richmond, Margaret R. and Robert M. Freeman Library, VMFA Archives, Richmond, Virginia, VA12.04.4.001

Hanne Darboven (1941–2009)
Month III (March), 1974
Ink on 31 pieces of transparentized paper
66½ × 70 × 1½ inches (168.9 × 177.8 × 3.8 cm), installed
The Museum of Modern Art, New York. The Judith Rothschild Foundation Contemporary Drawings Collection Gift, 2005

Hanne Darboven (1941–2009)
Untitled, 1969
Offset lithograph
4 × 6 inches (10.2 × 15.2 cm)
Collection of Jennie C. Jones

Julius Eastman (1940–1990)
Score for *Stay On It*, 1973
12 × 18 inches (30.5 × 45.7 cm)
Distributed by G. Schirmer and
Wise Music Group
Collection of Jennie C. Jones

Fred Eversley (1941–2025)
Untitled (parabolic lens), 1970
Cast polyester
19½ × 19½ × 5⅝ inches (49.5 ×
49.5 × 14.3 cm)
Private collection

Charles Gaines (b. 1944)
Incomplete Text #6 "E," 1978–79
Photostat (a); pen and colored
inks, correction fluid, and
graphite pencil on paper (b); pen
and colored inks and graphite
pencil on paper (c), 3 sheets
27⅝ × 59¾ inches (70.2 ×
151.8 cm)
Whitney Museum of American
Art, New York; Gift of Meredith
Palmer in honor of Adam D.
Weinberg, 2010.226a-c

Carmen Herrera (1915–2022)
Borealis, 1966/2016
Acrylic and aluminum
26 × 60 × 5⅛ inches (66 ×
152.4 × 13 cm)
Collection of Mr. and Mrs. Lee
Broughton

Carmen Herrera (1915–2022)
Pavanne (Green), 1967/2016
Acrylic and aluminum
35⅞ × 35⅞ × 23⅞ inches
(91.1 × 91.1 × 60.6 cm)
Edition 1 of 1 + 1 AP
Courtesy of Lisson Gallery

Carmen Herrera (1915–2022)
Untitled, 2015
Acrylic and pencil on paper
24½ × 36½ inches (62.2 ×
92.7 cm)
Courtesy of Lisson Gallery

Jennie C. Jones (b. 1968)
Standing and Moving #1–2, 2024
Collage and acrylic on paper
25¾ × 19¾ inches (65.4 ×
50.2 cm) each
Courtesy Alexander Gray
Associates, New York

Jennie C. Jones (b. 1968)
Standing and Moving #6, 2024
Collage and acrylic on paper
25¾ × 19¾ inches (65.4 ×
50.2 cm)
Courtesy Alexander Gray
Associates, New York

Ellsworth Kelly (1923–2015)
Talmont, 1951
Oil on canvas
26 × 64½ inches (66 × 163.8 cm)
Collection of Jack Shear

Agnes Martin (1912–2004)
Untitled, 1963
Pen and ink, brush and ink,
and wash on paper
11¹³⁄₁₆ × 11¹⁵⁄₁₆ inches (30 ×
30.3 cm)
Whitney Museum of American
Art, New York; Gift of the
Walter family in honor of May E.
Walter 91.29

Agnes Martin (1912–2004)
Benevolence, 2001
Acrylic and graphite on canvas
60 × 60 inches (152.4 × 152.4 cm)
Dia Art Foundation; gift of
the artist

Louise Nevelson (1899–1988)
Untitled, 1972
Collage on paper
29¹⁵⁄₁₆ × 20 inches (76 × 50.8 cm)
Whitney Museum of American
Art, New York; Gift of Jean and
Howard Lipman 97.113.3

Louise Nevelson (1899–1988)
Untitled, 1972
Paper collage and colored
pencil on board
29¹⁵⁄₁₆ × 20 inches (76 × 50.8 cm)
Whitney Museum of American
Art, New York; Gift of Jean and
Howard Lipman 97.113.4

Lorraine O'Grady (1934–2024)
Cutting Out CONYT 26,
1977/2017
Letterpress printing on Japanese
paper, cutout, collage on laid
paper
41¾ × 29¾ inches (106 ×
75.6 cm)
Courtesy Alexander Gray
Associates, New York

Benjamin Patterson (1934–2016)
String Music, 1960
Facsimile, printed 2025 from an
original black ink on folded paper
10¾ × 16 inches (27.3 × 40.6 cm)
Getty Research Institute, Los
Angeles (890164)

Benjamin Patterson (1934–2016)
Variations for Double-Bass
(page 1), ca. 1962
Facsimile, printed 2025 from
an original typed carbon paper
transfer on paper
11 × 8⁹⁄₁₆ inches (27.9 × 21.7 cm)
The Museum of Modern Art. The
Gilbert and Lila Silverman Fluxus
Collection Gift, 2640.2008.a

Benjamin Patterson (1934–2016)
Variations for Double-Bass
and *Duo for Voice and a String
Instrument*, performed during
*Kleines Sommerfest: Après
John Cage*, Galerie Parnass
Wuppertal, West Germany,
June 9, 1962
Facsimile, printed 2025 from
original gelatin silver prints
on board
10⅞ × 7¹¹⁄₁₆ inches (27.6 ×
19.5 cm)
The Museum of Modern Art. The
Gilbert and Lila Silverman Fluxus
Collection Gift, 3158.2008.a

Adrian Piper (b. 1948)
Untitled, 1969
Offset lithograph
4 × 6 inches (10.2 × 15.2 cm)
Collection of Jennie C. Jones

Adrian Piper (b. 1948)
My Calling (Card) #1 (Reactive Guerilla Performance for Bars and Discos), 1986
Offset lithograph
2 1/16 × 3 1/2 inches (5.2 × 8.9 cm)
Collection of Jennie C. Jones

Martin Puryear (b. 1941)
Métissage/Camouflage, 2016
Woodcut on Torinko paper
35 5/8 × 47 3/4 inches (90.5 × 121.3 cm)
Courtesy Universal Limited Art Editions

Mavis Pusey (1928–2019)
Untitled (Abstract), 1963
Lithograph on wove paper
10 5/8 × 14 15/16 inches (27 × 38 cm)
National Gallery of Art, Washington, Reba and Dave Williams Collection, Gift of Reba and Dave Williams, 2008.115.3995

Mavis Pusey (1928–2019)
Quiet Movement, 1965
Etching and aquatint on paper
12 × 9 inches (30.5 × 22.9 cm)
Petrucci Family Foundation Collection of African American Art

Mavis Pusey (1928–2019)
Study, ca. 1970
Lithograph on wove paper
15 1/8 × 20 3/4 inches (38.4 × 52.7 cm)
Virginia Museum of Fine Arts, Richmond, Aldine S. Hartman Endowment Fund and National Endowment for the Arts Fund for American Art, 2022.58

Alma Thomas (1891–1978)
Red Tree in High Winter, 1968
Acrylic and graphite on canvas
24 × 34 1/4 inches (61 × 87 cm)
Colby College Museum of Art, Waterville, Maine. Museum purchase from the Jere Abbott Acquisitions Fund, 2017.383

Mildred Thompson (1936–2003)
Wood Picture, ca. 1966
Found wood and acrylic paint
39 3/8 × 27 1/8 × 2 3/8 inches (100 × 68.9 × 6 cm)
New Orleans Museum of Art, Museum Purchase, Leah Chase Fund, 2016.49

Mildred Thompson (1936–2003)
Untitled, 1969
Paper collage
8 1/8 × 8 5/8 inches (20.6 × 21.9 cm)
Private collection

Rose Tripoli (b. 1942)
Untitled (Robert Blackburn and Benjamin Wigfall in Doorway of CV [Communications Village]), ca. 1974–76
Silver gelatin print on wove paper
9 15/16 × 7 7/8 inches (25.2 × 20 cm)
Virginia Museum of Fine Arts, Richmond, Arthur and Margaret Glasgow Endowment, 2022.239

Anne Truitt (1921–2004)
Spring Dryad, 1975
Acrylic on wood
76 × 13 × 8 inches (193 × 33 × 20.3 cm)
Collection of Steve Elmendorf

Anne Truitt (1921–2004)
Harvest Shade, 1996
Acrylic on wood
60 1/4 × 5 1/2 × 4 inches (153 × 14 × 10.2 cm)
Private collection

Anne Truitt (1921–2004)
Sound Nine, 2003
Acrylic on paper
19 1/2 × 19 1/2 inches (49.5 × 49.5 cm)
Collection of Steve Elmendorf

Anne Truitt (1921–2004)
Sound Fourteen, 2003
Acrylic on paper
19 1/4 × 19 3/4 inches (48.9 × 50.2 cm)
Collection of Steve Elmendorf

Jack Whitten (1939–2018)
Psee II, 1978
Acrylic on canvas
17 × 16 inches (43.2 × 40.6 cm)
Collection of Lizbeth and George Krupp

Benjamin Wigfall (1930–2017)
Nine Part Black Theme, 1971
Etching on Arches wove paper
30 × 22 1/4 inches (76.2 × 56.5 cm)
Virginia Museum of Fine Arts, Richmond, Arthur and Margaret Glasgow Endowment, 2022.214

Zarina (1937–2020)
Wall, 1969
Relief print from collaged wood, printed in burnt umber on Indian handmade paper
21 7/8 × 28 inches (55.6 × 71.1 cm)
Whitney Museum of American Art, New York; Purchase, with funds from the Print Committee 2011.10

All unidentified installation images are from the exhibitions *Jennie C. Jones: A Line When Broken Begins Again* and *Other Octaves: Curated by Jennie C. Jones*, Pulitzer Arts Foundation, St. Louis September 5, 2025–February 1, 2026 Photographs by Suzy Gorman: pp. 1, 22–23, 58–59; Alise O'Brien: pp. 6, 112–13, 119. © Pulitzer Arts Foundation and the photographers

Courtesy Alexander Gray Associates, New York © 2025 Jennie C. Jones: pp. 9, 13, 14, 25, 26, 29, 30, 32, 33, 34, 43, 44–45, 46–47, 48, 73, 74–75. © Ellsworth Kelly Foundation: pp. 61, 62. © Ellsworth Kelly Foundation, Photo © Katrin Schilling: p. 17. Choreography © Courtesy of the Estate of Trisha Brown, Digital Image © The Museum of Modern Art/Licensed by SCALA/Art Resource, NY: p. 53. © Estate of Carmen Herrera, Courtesy Lisson Gallery: pp. 66, 67, 68. © 2025 The Estate of Robert Morris/Artists Rights Society (ARS), New York. Photo Courtesy Castelli Gallery: p. 12. © 2025 Estate of Louise Nevelson/Artists Rights Society (ARS), New York, Digital image Whitney Museum of American Art/Licensed by Scala, 2025 © Photo Scala, Florence: pp. 102, 105. © 2025 Estate of Mavis Pusey/Artists Rights Society (ARS), New York: p. 99. © 2025 Estate of Mavis Pusey/ Artists Rights Society (ARS), New York, Courtesy National Gallery of Art: p. 100. © 2025 Estate of Mavis Pusey/Artists Rights Society (ARS), New York, © Virginia Museum of Fine Arts. Photo: Troy Wilkinson: p. 101. © 2025 Estate of Alma Thomas (Courtesy of the Hart Family)/Artists Rights Society (ARS), New York: p. 70. © Estate of Anne Truitt/Bridgeman Images: p. 77. © Estate of Anne Truitt/Bridgeman Images, Courtesy Matthew Marks Gallery: pp. 54, 76, 78, 79. © Fred Eversley. Photo: Suzy Gorman, p. 87. © Charles Gaines. Courtesy the artist and Hauser & Wirth, Digital image Whitney Museum of American Art/ Licensed by Scala, 2025 © Photo Scala, Florence: pp. 108–9. © Hanne Darboven Stiftung, Hamburg/ Artists Rights Society (ARS), New York 2025, Digital Image © The Museum of Modern Art/ Licensed by SCALA/Art Resource, NY: p. 110. © Agnes Martin Foundation, New York/Artists Rights Society (ARS), New York. Image courtesy Dia Art Foundation: p. 80. © Agnes Martin Foundation, New York/Artists Rights Society (ARS), New York. Digital image Whitney Museum of American Art/Licensed by Scala, 2025 © Photo Scala, Florence: p. 85. © Rose Tripoli Mueller, © Virginia Museum of Fine Arts: 98 (right). © 2018 by Music Sales Corporation (ASCAP) and Eastman Music Publishing Co. (ASCAP). All rights administered by Music Sales Corporation (ASCAP). International Copyright Secured. All Rights Reserved. Used by Permission. Warning: Unauthorized reproduction of this publication is prohibited by Federal law and subject to criminal prosecution: p. 93. © 2025 Lorraine O'Grady/Artists Rights Society (ARS), New York, Courtesy Alexander Gray Associates, New York: p. 111. © Benjamin Patterson, courtesy the Estate of Benjamin Patterson, Getty Research Institute, Los Angeles (890164): p. 92. © Benjamin Patterson, courtesy the Estate of Benjamin Patterson, Digital Image © The Museum of Modern Art/Licensed by SCALA/Art Resource, NY: pp. 90, 91. © Jan Persson/CTSIMAGES: p. 19. © 2025 Pulitzer Arts Foundation and Suzy Gorman: pp. 1, 22–23, 58–59. © 2025 Pulitzer Arts Foundation and Alise O'Brien: pp. 6, 28, 36–37, 39, 40, 50, 112–13, 119. © Martin Puryear, Courtesy Matthew Marks Gallery and Universal Limited Art Editions: p. 107. © The Mildred Thompson Estate. Courtesy Galerie Lelong & Co., New York: p. 88. © The Mildred Thompson Estate. Courtesy Galerie Lelong & Co., New York. Photography by Roman Alokhin, courtesy New Orleans Museum of Art: p. 89. © 2025 Jack Whitten Estate/Artists Rights Society (ARS), New York, Courtesy Alexander Gray Associates, New York: p. 96. © Benjamin Wigfall Estate. © Virginia Museum of Fine Arts. Photo: Travis Fullerton: pp. 97, 98 (left). © Zarina, Courtesy the artist and Luhring Augustine, New York, Digital image Whitney Museum of American Art/Licensed by Scala, 2025 © Photo Scala, Florence: p. 95.

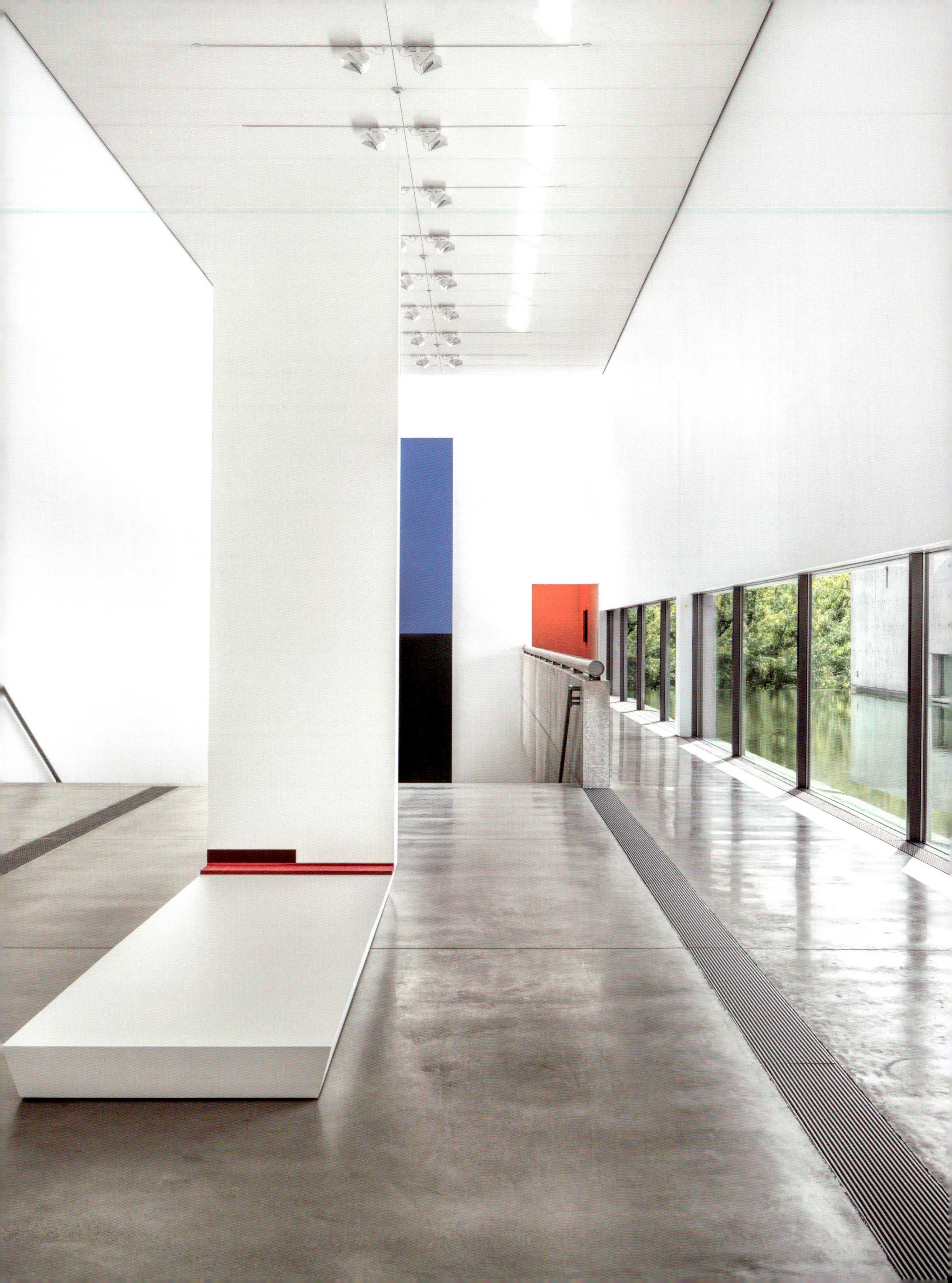

This book is published on the occasion of the exhibitions *A Line When Broken Begins Again*, organized by Stephanie Weissberg, senior curator, with Heather Alexis Smith, assistant curator, Pulitzer Arts Foundation, and *Other Octaves: Curated by Jennie C. Jones.*

Pulitzer Arts Foundation
September 5, 2025–February 1, 2026

Published by
Pulitzer Arts Foundation
3716 Washington Boulevard
St. Louis, MO 63108
pulitzerarts.org

Distributed by ARTBOOK | D.A.P.
75 Broad Street, Suite 630
New York, NY 10004
artbook.com

Produced by Marquand Books, Seattle
marquandbooks.com

Editorial and creative direction: Donna Wingate
Editor: Susan Higman Larsen
Publication coordinator: Heather Alexis Smith
Proofreader: Carrie Wicks
Designer: Katy Nelson
Layout: Ryan Polich
Typesetter: Maggie Lee
Color management: I/O Color, Seattle

Printed and bound in Italy at Printer Trento S.p.A.

Frontispiece and page 119:
Jennie C. Jones
Point of Perspective, 2025
Wood, MDF, acrylic paint, and architectural felt
142 × 36 × 148 inches (360.7 × 91.4 × 375.9 cm)
Courtesy Alexander Gray Associates, New York,
© 2025 Jennie C. Jones

The following previously published articles
© Jennie C. Jones:
Jennie C. Jones, "Alma's Mark," in *Alma Thomas* (The Studio Museum in Harlem; The Frances Young Tang Teaching Museum and Art Gallery at Skidmore College; and DelMonico Books/Prestel, 2016), 147.

Jennie C. Jones, "Blue Turning Gray Over You," *Art in America*, March 2016, 54–55.

Jennie C. Jones, "The Price of Tenderness," in *Agnes Martin: Independence of Mind* (Radius Books, 2022), 87–92.

Jennie C. Jones, "Louise Nevelson: The Utility of Recomposing and the Necessity of Blackness," in *Louise Nevelson: I Must Recompose the Environment* (Inventory Press, 2018), 79–81.

Library of Congress Control Number:
2025946105
ISBN: 978-0-9976901-8-7

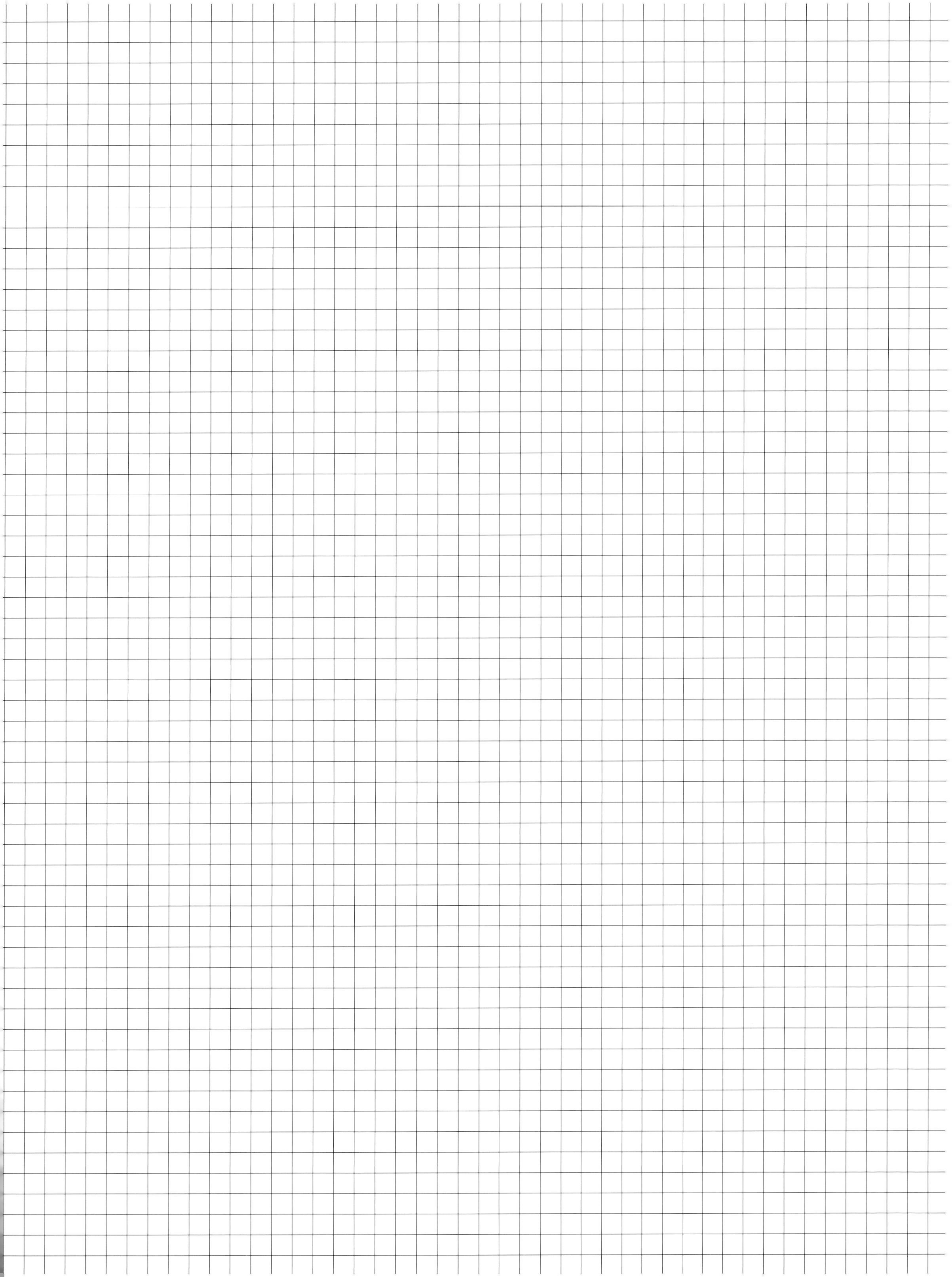

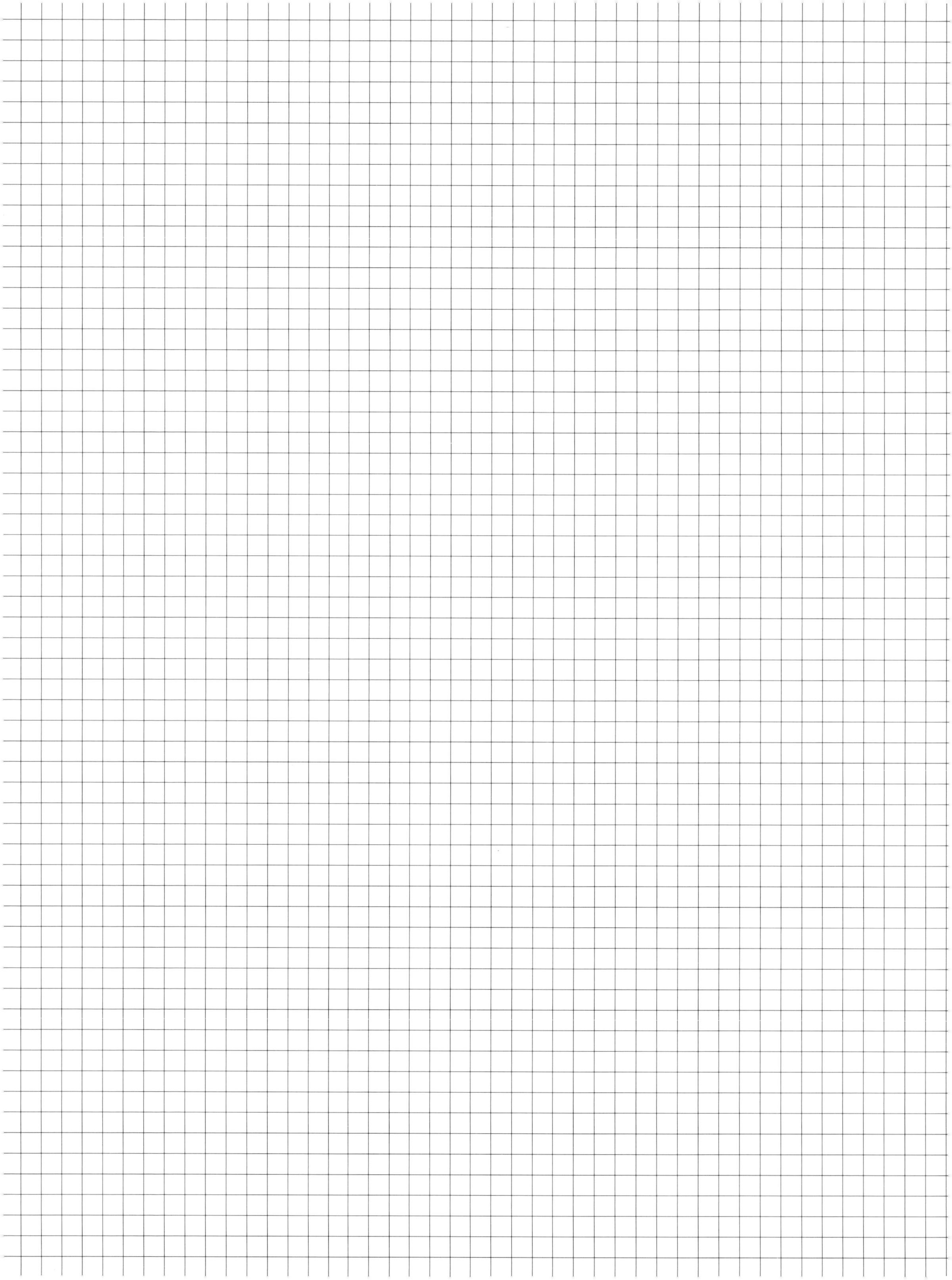